HOW FAITH GROWS
Faith Development and Christian Education

National Society/Church House Publishing
Church House, Great Smith Street, London SW1P 3NZ

The National Society

The National Society (Church of England) for Promoting Religious Education is the voluntary body, founded in 1811, which established the first network of schools in England and Wales based on the national Church. It now supports all those involved in Christian education—diocesan education teams, teachers, governors, clergy, students and parents—with the resources of its RE Centres, archives, courses and conferences. The Society publishes a wide range of books, pamphlets and audio-visual items, and two magazines, *Crosscurrent* and *Together*. It can give legal and administrative advice for schools and colleges and award grants for Church school building projects.

The Society works in close association with the General Synod Board of Education, and with the Division for Education of the Church in Wales, but greatly values the independent status which enables it to take initiatives in developing new work. The Society has a particular concern for Christian goals and values in education as a whole.

For details of corporate, associate and individual membership of the Society contact: The Promotions Secretary, The National Society, Church House, Great Smith Street, London SW1P 3NZ. Telephone 071-222 1672.

ISBN 0 7151 4809 5

Published 1991 for the General Synod Board of Education
jointly by the National Society and Church House Publishing.

Cover design by Bill Bruce
Some illustrations by Neil Pinchbeck
Printed in England by The Campfield Press

Contents

Abbreviations

Works by James Fowler in the following:

BABC	*Becoming Adult, Becoming Christian*
CA	*Clinical Handbook of Pastoral Counseling*
EIRE	*Emerging Issues in Religious Education*
FDEC	*Faith Development in Early Childhood*
FDF	*Faith Development and Fowler*
FDPC	*Faith Development and Pastoral Care*
FSM	*Toward Moral and Religious Maturity*
G	*The Foundation*
LM	*Life Maps*
M	*Manual for Faith Development Research*
MSDF	*Moral Development, Moral Education, and Kohlberg*
N	*Network Paper No. 31*
PF	*The Perkins Journal, 33 (1979)*
SF	*Stages of Faith*
SFALC	*Faith Development in the Adult Life Cycle*

Works by John Westerhoff:

WOCHF	*Will our Children Have Faith?*

Full bibliographical details are to be found in the Booklist (pp89ff).

A NOTE ON LANGUAGE

It is difficult to avoid sexist language when writing in English without using cumbersome and unnatural phrases and sentences. Throughout this book the word 'she' is intended to imply 'she or he', and 'he' to cover 'he or she'. The Working Party hopes that this is an acceptable convention if used in both forms.

Foreword

The team who have written *How Faith Grows,* and especially Dr Jeff Astley who has been editor and principal writer, have done a lively and faithful job of communicating faith development research and theory. They minted fresh language for communicating complex ideas in straightforward and engaging ways. In addition, they have taken up and discussed some of the critical questions raised by this body of work in very helpful ways. Finally, the authors have made fruitful steps toward informing the imaginations of religious educators with the implications of faith development studies for the work of churches and schools. Their efforts in the last third of the book parallel some of the central thrusts of my 1991 book, *Weaving the New Creation* (San Francisco, Harper and Row).

I am indebted to these colleagues for the seriousness and depth with which they have taken on my thought, and for the real contribution they are making to its critical and constructive appropriation in the United Kingdom. This book is a worthy successor and companion to *Children in the Way.* May both books contribute to the strengthening and extension of informed passion for formation and nurture in faith for children, youth and adults.

James W. Fowler
Emory University, Atlanta, Georgia, USA

Preface

This book originated from the discussions of a Working Party set up by the Church of England General Synod Board of Education to evaluate research into faith development and its implications for Christian education.

Jeff Astley has served as the editor and main author of the book, drawing on contributions from other members of the Working Party. The text has been discussed and approved for publication by the Faith Development Working Party, the membership of which is given below:

The Revd Dr Jeff Astley, Director, North of England Institute for Christian Education

The Revd Derek Atkinson, Director, Exeter Christian Education and Resources Centre

Miss Jenny Holmes, Adviser in Religious Education, Diocese of Salisbury

Dr Fred Hughes, Senior Lecturer in Religious Studies, Cheltenham and Gloucester College of Higher Education (Chairman)

Mrs Dorothy Jamal, Children's Officer, Board of Education, General Synod of the Church of England

Mr Steve Pearce, Adviser in Children's Work, Diocese of Southwell

Dr Marion Smith, formerly Senior Lecturer in Religious Studies, Roehampton Institute of Higher Education.

The Working Party would particularly like to express its thanks to the following:

Professor James Fowler for his enthusiastic support for this writing project, his permission to use various diagrams and exercises, and for contributing the Foreword;

The North of England Institute for Christian Education, and particularly its secretary Mrs Dorothy Greenwell, for undertaking most of the typing;

Cheltenham and Gloucester College of Higher Education, for the use of its premises and administrative support;

The Trusts who are supporting the activities of the Working Party, including the ongoing research programme:

St Christopher's Educational Trust
St Hild and St Bede Trust
St Luke's College Foundation
Sarum St Michael Educational Charity.

HarperCollins Publishers (New York) for permission to quote from James Fowler's *Stages of Faith* (1976), and to reproduce illustrations from the book cover and text; Word Incorporated (Dallas, Texas) for permission to quote from *Life Maps* by James Fowler and Sam Keen (1978); Augsburg Fortress (Minneapolis) for permission to quote from James Fowler, *Faith Development and Pastoral Care* (1987); Paulist Press (Mahwah, New Jersey) for permission to duplicate a diagram from Fowler's article in *Emerging Issues in Religious Education* (edited by Gloria Durka and Joanmarie Smith, 1976); and the Editor of *The Month* for permission to re-use material from Marion Smith's article 'Developments in Faith' (July 1983);

Introduction: The Way of Faith

In 1988 The National Society and Church House Publishing published the Report of the Church of England's Board of Education entitled *Children in the Way*. The ambiguity in that title was intended. The major model for Christian learning that was commended in the Report was that of a journey or pilgrimage, learning Christ 'along the Way'. But children and young people—and often some adult learners as well—often seem to clergy and others in the Church to be in the way in a more vulgar sense. They are the people we trip over as they untidily block our own spiritual, vocational or career progress.

Children in the Way has been widely read and has had some influence in Church circles. One of its recommendations (4.1 on p91) was that the Church should make an 'appraisal of the research into faith development and its implications for Christian nurture'. In acting upon this recommendation the General Synod's Board of Education appointed a small group to undertake this work. This Working Party has met many times to discuss the faith development research of James Fowler and his associates, together with other literature relevant to this research. It is also engaged in some practical faith development research of its own, with the help of grants from various charitable sources.

At this stage the Working Party believes that an introduction to and reflection on faith development and its implications might be of use to those people in the churches who have an interest in the pastoral care and Christian education of children, youth and adults. This book is aimed at them and at all those who welcomed the earlier Report—including a wide range of lay people, particularly those who are parents, as well as clergy, teachers and diocesan advisers.

We have attempted in this book to keep the discussion at as straightforward a level as possible. But we have also tried to do justice to the details of faith development theory, and the criticisms that have been made of it. References to key texts are given throughout, together with notes that make more technical points or refer the reader to related literature. These may, of course, be ignored by those with a more general interest, but we hope that by including them the book can be of use to a wider audience and that our exposition and arguments may be checked and followed up by any who wish to do so.

We should pin our colours to the mast at the outset. It is our view that faith development theory offers an illuminating and practically-relevant contribution to the practice of the Church, particularly in the areas of Christian education and pastoral care. We are not uncritical of the approach, however, and hope that we have provided here an introduction that is both accessible and judicious and which will help others to decide for themselves how seriously to take the theory.

Our account is of the *way of faith*. It is about what constitutes faith, and how that faith develops. It is about the ways in which we make sense of and relate to 'life, the universe, and everything'—and especially God—in our particular journeying as children and young people, and through our adult years. It is the story of human development and growth in the way of faith.

1

What is Faith?

THE FORM AND CONTENT OF FAITH

'Jane' was 79 years of age when interviewed; she had led a very full life. Here is a little of the interview with her[1]:

> *Interviewer: Could you say what it is that makes life meaningful for you?*
> *Jane: I think it is knowing, I do believe every one of us is put here with possibilities and for a purpose or for a choice of purposes. There is a place always for everyone, and I feel we have to find that place or one of them, there obviously are alternatives, and as long as we feel we have a purpose, then we feel close to God. I always have a little picture of when you accept him completely: it's like you have been sitting in the audience, you then step up on the platform and sit beside him and try to look at the world as he is trying, as he is looking at it, just try to get alongside and then you can see further I think.*
> *Interviewer: That's a lovely image.*
> *Jane: Well I do wonder sometimes. It sounds a bit cheeky but it seems to work.*

Not everyone speaks like that about their faith! 'When I was a child', wrote St Paul, 'I spoke like a child, I thought like a child, I reasoned like a child' (1 Corinthians 13.11, *RSV*). This (deliberately partial) text may be used as an introduction to what we hope to say about faith development. Whatever else Paul may or may not have meant by it, the quotation implies that children think differently from adults. This does not just mean that they think about different things or have different ideas—that the *content* of their thinking is different. It also means that the *way* they think is often different from the way an adult thinks. And what is true of their thinking is true also of the way they view other people; the way they value; the way they make sense of the world; and the way they feel. As the *New English Bible* translates our text: 'When I was a child, my speech, my outlook and my thoughts were all childish.'

Those who work in the area of 'faith development' bring together all these activities—thinking, valuing, feeling, making sense—under the broad category of 'faith'. Faith, for them, although it has the

1

grammatical form of a noun, is to be thought of rather as a verb. It is not something we have, but something we do. We might even call it 'faithing'. St Paul's text may then be rewritten: 'When I was a child, I *faithed* as a child.' Or, to put it in James Fowler's own words:

> One who becomes Christian in childhood may indeed remain Christian all of his or her life. But one's *way* of being Christian will need to deepen, expand, and be reconstituted several times in the pilgrimage of faith. (*FSM* 79)[2]

This is the claim that lies at the heart of faith development theory: that there is a development through childhood *and* adulthood (the Pauline text needs expanding here) in our way of being in faith.

We may be misled by the text from St Paul, however, if we take it to imply that this development involves our completely giving up a child's perspective as we adopt adult ways. (The quotation from 1 Corinthians 13 continues in the *RSV*, 'when I became a man, I gave

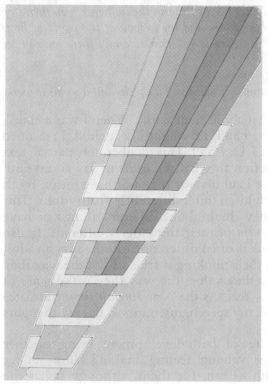

up childish ways'.) This change is, rather, a matter of transformation—a change of form—of what is already there. If the metaphor of a staircase is adopted (and it has its limitations) then we are thinking here of a *spiral* staircase on which step fifteen is directly above step ten and step five. As we ascend to the higher step it may be said both that we are in the same place, and that we have moved on. But perhaps the image of lenses or filters is a better one. The diagram shown here appears on the cover of James Fowler's *Stages of Faith*:

The adult's beliefs, feelings and relations are like a coloured image formed as a beam of light passes through a bank of filters (from lower left to upper right in this picture). Many of the colours in the image have been contributed by the coloured lenses of earlier stages of the person's life. The child's faith is still there, making a contribution to the adult's faith, but it is a contribution that is amended and adapted through the glass of later ways of faith.

For Fowler and his colleagues, 'faith' is primarily about *making meaning*. It 'has to do with the making, maintenance, and transformation of human meaning' (*FSM* 53). As such it includes our knowing, valuing, interpreting, understanding, experiencing and feeling. It is about giving positive value to attitudes and ideals, and finding significant patterns and connections within the world and within oneself. What Fowler means by faith is essentially an orientation of the person to life, our 'way-of-being-in-relation' to what we believe to be ultimate (*LM* 24). It is a disposition, a stance, 'a way of moving into and giving form and coherence to life' (*LM* 24). In a fine phrase, Fowler talks about faith in terms of our 'way of moving into the force field of life' (*SF* 4). Faith is a 'way of leaning into life, of meeting and shaping our experience' (unpublished lecture handout). Like a mariner on the prow of his ship leaning into the wind, our position and posture determine not only what we see but whether we shall keep our footing.

In his account Fowler draws on the work of several theologians and students of religion[3] who have distinguished faith from both religion and belief. Faith here is not just a matter of holding beliefs about God or other people, of assenting to propositions. It is a much more passionate and self-involving affair, an orientation of the whole person—heart as well as mind. Here *'cognition* and *affection* are interwoven' (*G* 8). 'To "have faith" is to be related to someone or something in such a way that our heart is invested, our caring is committed, our hope is focused on the other' (*LM* 18); 'knowing and valuing are . . . inseparable' (*EIRE* 193). In Sharon Parks's words: ' "Faithing" . . . is the composing of the heart's resting place', for 'affect has an ordering power'.[4]

This pledging of allegiance (compare the old wedding service's 'plighting our troth') is obviously not just restricted to religious objects of faith, nor is it the prerogative solely of religious people. Fowler identifies faith as a human universal. He claims that everyone shows some sort of commitment of this nature—some sort of 'faith'. Everyone, we might say, 'believes *in*' someone or other, something or other. Our hearts inevitably rest somewhere. We all worship—give supreme worth to—some god, whether that be our new toy (Teddy bear-shaped or Porsche-shaped) or 'the Lord who is high and lifted up'. Some people sometimes have many such gods, all more or less at the same level of devotion. They are truly 'polytheists'. Sometimes one of these 'deities' is given a status that is head and shoulders above the other objects of devotion: power perhaps, or family. Others at other times act as if there is only one *real* god for them. This is their one true God, who is so much more worshipful than any other focus of their lives that these lesser 'goods' aren't really 'gods' at all. This is 'monotheism'.[5] So there are many different ways for people to be in faith, but they can all be said to have faith.

Fowler writes: 'The opposite of faith, as we consider it here, is not doubt. Rather, the opposite of faith is nihilism'—that is an inability to image *anything* in which one believes—'and despair about the possibility of even negative meaning' (*SF* 31). So one can have faith in a universe that is chaotic, impersonal and indifferent. This would be a form of 'atheistic faith'. Someone who had suffered a *complete* loss of faith would not even believe in or be related to that view of Reality. As the Preface to *Life Maps* puts it: 'Anyone not about to kill himself lives by faith' (*LM* 1).[6]

In faith we are in relation both horizontally and vertically, as it were. Horizontally we relate to other people. Vertically we also relate, as these other people do, 'to the ultimate conditions and depths of existence' (*G* 6). This is my (our) idea or image of an *ultimate environment*: that which we take to be ultimate, about which we are 'ultimately concerned', what Fowler sometimes calls 'the big picture'. Fowler is using here an ecological metaphor. All organisms live in relation to their immediate environment—a pond, a stone wall or a hedgerow. Human beings can look further afield in their relationships and at length come to the far horizons of all their interactions with the universe. This is *our* environment, and human faith is 'a matter of composing an image of [this] ultimate environment' (*MSDF* 136).

Faith thus has a *content*. That content is made up of *what* (and *who*) we value, hold dear, commit ourselves to, revere, serve, align ourselves to and fear. Fowler calls these our 'centres of value' and 'images and realities of power'. 'The centres of value and power that have god value for us . . . are those that confer meaning and worth on us and promise to sustain us in a dangerous world of power' (*SF* 18). Along with them the content of our faith includes epic tales, homely wisdom and

4

analogies for our lives, poetic images and mythologies that we tell ourselves and through which we interpret our own lives and our own stories. Fowler calls these our 'master stories' or 'core stories'. 'In Jewish and Christian terms', Fowler writes, 'the ultimate environment is expressed with the symbol "Kingdom of God". In this way of seeing, *God* is the centre of power and value which unifies and gives character to the ultimate environment' (*FSM* 56). For these religions, the master stories are stories about God's relationship to his creation.

Most people would talk of this ultimate Reality as having been 'discovered' or 'received' through religious experience or revelation. But Fowler puts it differently. Like many psychologists he speaks of (our image of) Reality as being 'constructed' and 'maintained', 'composed' and 'constituted', by us (*G* 6f, *FSM* 57f, *EIRE* 194). The way *we see* things (including God's revelation) is our only access to the way *things are*. We 'construe' and 'constitute' our Reality. We may affirm that God is, or is not, 'out there'. Ultimate value and power may be thought of as independent of our valuing and serving. But whatever 'really' exists, whatever is really ultimate, is a Reality that is known to us only in our portraying of it. That portrait is inevitably painted by our paintbrush, using colours from our paintbox. And the brush and the pigments are features of faith. God is only experienced and understood when *the God* becomes *our god,* as an object (content) of our faith.

It must be stressed that Fowler and others who adopt such a view are *not* suggesting that ' "meaning" need have no objective referent in "reality" or in what *is*' (*FDF* 284). They are not denying that there is something 'out there'. They are insisting, however, that our understanding of Reality and God is something that we do, in our human way and from our human perspective. As human beings we are naturally meaning-makers. It is built in to us. God has made us like this, so that we naturally make sense of our—and his—Reality. Truth, Reality, Meaning, the World and God are in a sense 'givens'. They are given to us. But in receiving them—experiencing and knowing them—they also become 'the work of human hands'.

So much for the content of faith—the *what* of faith. It is invariably there. There could be no faith without it. Christian education and preaching has traditionally paid considerable attention to this content. But it is not all that can be said about faith, and it is not James Fowler's primary concern. His interest is in the *how* of faith: its *form*, rather than its content—faith 'as a dynamic but structured process' (*EIRE* 192).

Underlying the differing contents of people's faith, Fowler's research claims to have found what he calls 'the inner structures or form of faith-knowing', 'the *pattern* of emotion-thought' (*G* 9). These are the '*patterns* or *structures* of thought, of valuing, and of constitutive-knowing' (knowing that in part constitutes what is known) (*FSM* 65).

In the pilgrimage of faith, along the Way of the Christian journey, we may now understand the phrase 'the way of faith' as the way in which people hold their faith: 'the way of being that is faith' (*BABC* 52). It is made up of the processes or operations of human believing, valuing, understanding and relating. These together constitute *how* our faith is held.

Of course the contents of our faith change over time. At one time our mother's breast is our 'ultimate environment'. Later our world is made up of a wider circle of family and others with their (= our) ideas about what is true and good. At one time, perhaps, I imagine God as an elderly Superman or Father Christmas figure: genial and all-powerful, probably white and male. Perhaps later I will speak of God as 'infinite mind'; of heaven as 'a state not a place'; of ultimate truth and value as 'God's own thoughts'. Often as we grow up our ideals, *what* we really 'believe in' passionately, will undergo a conversion. Our faith will have changed in its *content*. From childhood to adolescence and through adulthood it is inevitably subject to this sort of change of content. But these changes are not what Fowler has researched, although they affect and are affected by the changes he is really interested in. His thesis is that there is a change and development in the *how* of faith, in its form: 'qualitative transformations in the person's structures or patterns of thinking, valuing, committing and believing' (*EIRE* 200).

Now it is both illuminating and risky to attempt to separate form and content in this way. Both, we should note, are abstractions. Concrete reality—whether physical or human—always consists of 'formed content'. There is no such thing as pure form (except in geometrical thinking), nor of pure ('un-formed', 'formless') content. Even the molten steel which makes the poker takes the form of the crucible in which it is temporarily held. With our mind, however, we can separate the two, at least to an extent. But it is an open question as to how far we—or Fowler—can get with this thought experiment.[7]

An example and a metaphor may show what this concentration on the form of faith looks like. At one time a person may have a view of God that is explicitly or implicitly qualified by the words 'as my vicar says' or 'as my friends believe'. At another time the same theological painting (content) might be put into a different enclosing frame (form)—the frame of a consciously self-chosen belief. We may imagine this as having different mottoes inscribed around its edge. These now read 'as I choose to believe' or 'either God is this or he is nothing'. At yet another time the frame might be more complicated, perhaps constructed with movable sections that open on to and connect with other frames. This new frame has new mottoes: 'God is like this, but others may also say . . .', 'This same God is spoken of in different ways by many different people', 'This truth is a small part of a greater truth', and so on. The analogy is imperfect, but it may help us to distinguish two parts of one reality: the content-painting and the form-frame. In a human life the form of faith will always have some influence on, and be influenced by, its content; yet we can distinguish content and form in faith as well. So it is possible for the same person to keep more or less the same theology over a period of time, while the way in which that theology is 'kept' changes radically.[8]

Fowler summarizes this notion of faith as form in terms of the changing ways in which:

(i) we experience ourselves, others and our world (as we construct them);

(ii) we relate to and are affected by the ultimate conditions of existence (as we construct them); and

(iii) we shape our lives' purposes and meanings, trusts and loyalties, in the light of what we imagine and understand about these ultimate conditions (cf. *SF* 92f).

This concept of faith, Fowler claims, is one that holds together the 'various interrelated dimensions of human knowing, valuing, committing and acting' and expresses itself in 'the making and maintaining of human meaning' (*loc. cit.*).

Thus 'faith', as we treat the term in this book and as Fowler understands it, is essentially a way of knowing, valuing, being committed to, and understanding life. Faith gives meaning to our lives. It relates us to one another and to what we take to be ultimate, *our* discerned life-context. Faith is not specific to, or limited to, any one religion. It is not necessarily religious at all and may have a wide range of different contents that can be religious or non-religious. Thus it may focus on God, Nirvana, the physical universe, money or Mummy. It is not, therefore, quite the same as what many Christians call 'The Faith' or 'Our Faith'. In the terms we are using here, those phrases refer to the content of (our) Christian faith. Content is not our primary topic here, although we acknowledge that it is sometimes difficult to separate it out. And it is faith-as-a-process, not faith-as-a-product, with which we are concerned in this book. *Our topic is the form of human faithing.* And Christian faith, according to Fowler, is 'the conversion and formation of human faith in and through relationship to God' which is mediated through Jesus, the Scriptures and teachings of the Church, and the Holy Spirit (*N* 1).

THE ASPECTS OF FAITH

In analysing the form of faith, Fowler discerns several *aspects* or elements within it. He thinks of these as 'windows' into faith, which help us to see the different operations that are at work—in an integrated, interrelated way—to make up a person's faith. In the one faith, then, there are many processes, each one directed towards a certain area of content. Of the seven aspects analysed by Fowler some 'express more clearly cognitive content' (that is content related to our thinking and judging, which produces our beliefs, opinions and knowledge-claims about Reality), whereas others 'represent psychosocial as well as cognitive content' (i.e. they relate to the self and others, in terms of how we feel about them as well as what we know about them) (*M* 55). The aspects of faith are complex skills and competences that work together and, as it were, feed off one another. We may think of them as 'facets of faith'. They are like the different facets of the one diamond that together make it a stone worth having, brilliant and beautiful. Or we may think of them as so many fibres wound together in a single piece of thread or string, closely related and mutually strengthening.

The relationship between these aspects is a topic worthy of further research. The interrelationships between some of them are fairly obvious, but Fowler does not trace all the connections very clearly. He does affirm, however, that they are all integral components of the one faith stance. Briefly they are concerned with:

(A) The way we think;

(B) Our ability to adopt another's perspective;

(C) The way we make moral judgements;

(D) How and where we set the limits to our 'community of faith';

(E) How and where we find authorities on which to rely;

(F) Our way of 'holding it all together', of forming a single 'world-view'; and

(G) Our understanding of and response to symbols.

We may now explore each of these aspects of faith in turn.

(A) Thinking

'When I was a child I thought as a child, but now . . .'

Conversations with children can seem very bizarre to an adult:

A four-year-old was chatting in a railway carriage: 'Grandma's gone to heaven, so Jesus will look after her . . . (after a pause) . . . Anyway she's buried.'

Twin brothers were arguing at the church social: 'You've got more juice than me.' 'Well the vicar gave me it.' The curate intervenes. 'You've both got the same amount, but John's glass is narrower. Look, Neil, I'll pour your juice into the same shaped glass.' Neil: 'See, I've got more now!'

9

The child listened patiently to a full explanation of Daddy's academic success and its career implications. After some prompting he was able to rehearse the main points, before adding: 'Yes, but now can I have a banana?'

Five-year-old Gill giggled when she thought of her aunt's death. Her mother asked why. 'I was thinking how funny Auntie Rose would look, without a body.' 'Why?' 'Well, with her arms and legs sticking out of her head.'[9]

The way we make sense of the world is partly determined by the way we think. Children often think about the same things as adults, sometimes understanding them in the same way. In these cases their thinking has the same content, but the *form* of that thinking can still be drastically different. Parents and teachers, particularly primary school teachers and those working with younger children in Church, are familiar with this from their own experience. Teachers in particular will know of the influential work of the great developmental psychologist Jean Piaget, who provided so much stimulus to research on the *patterns* of children's thinking and their development.[10] Religious education teachers will recall the popularization of Piaget's work in the much publicized—but in some ways ill-founded—claims of Ronald Goldman in the 1960s that children cannot properly think in an abstract way about religious concepts before the mental age of thirteen.[11] Certainly the thoughts of very young children (those with a 'mental age' of five years or less) often seem quite chaotic, jumping from one topic to another, ignoring what we would think of as the logical implications of what they say. Only later do many of them begin to think 'logically' at least in the sense that they develop the power to 'go into reverse' in their thinking, that is to trace inferences backwards as well as forwards—a skill that enables them to check the validity of their arguments. Even at this stage, however, their thoughts are focused normally on concrete (particular and observable) things. They are limited by the experiences they have had. Abstract (general and non-observable) ideas can often only be grasped, or some would say 'misunderstood', if they are translated into concrete imagery. They can only be processed or arranged in concrete ways. Some adults continue to operate in this way. Most people, however, begin properly to think abstractly and to be able to reflect on their own thinking ('to think about thinking') at some stage, usually by secondary school.

Some of the other aspects of faith are clearly intimately associated with our way of thinking. If faith contains an element relating to knowledge/beliefs/opinions, then the pattern of our thinking is an important strand within it. As that pattern changes and develops, so our way of faith will similarly evolve.[12]

(B) Perspective-taking

'When I was a child I saw others as a child sees them, but now . . .'

The phrase 'perspective-taking' labels our changing ability to adopt the perspective of other people. It is often said that other people don't really exist as separate beings for a young baby, they are seen as a part of the child herself. Only gradually, and painfully, is Mummy recognized as a different and—horror of horrors—uncontrollable personality.[13] As we change and mature our ability to see things from the perspective of other people increases. We become less 'egocentric' in our view of others. We may come to see that they are not always 'just like us'. Eventually we may even be able to extend this shifting of perspective to those people whom we recognize not to be a bit like us. If faith is in part a matter of how we relate to other people, then this pattern of awareness is an integral part of it. It is also perhaps relevant to the way we come to view 'the Other' we call God.

(C) Moral judging

'When I was a child I judged like a child, but now . . .'

Another strand or facet of faith is the way we make moral judgments. Children and adults commit themselves to a great variety of moral views about which actions are right or wrong, what things and people are good or bad. But this variety is not just a variety of content. It can also reflect different ways in which people make these judgements. Lawrence Kohlberg and others have distinguished several different forms of moral thinking, which they claim constitute stages that people move through as they develop.[14] An example should illustrate what this might mean. As a child's moral thinking changes we often find that he no longer judges an accident with big results (e.g. breaking a lot of crockery by opening a door behind which it had been placed unknown to him) as more heinous than a disobedient act with lesser consequences (breaking one cup while stealing a forbidden item from a cupboard).

According to the research claims, for the very young child moral rules really belong to parents and teachers, and the child understands right and wrong mainly in terms of what attracts rewards and punishments. Later on notions of reciprocal fairness develop. A conventional level of moral thinking follows, with the adolescent conforming to stereotypes of what is 'natural' or (later) obeying fixed rules for their own sake. In adult life ways of moral thinking may change further. At one stage right action is defined in terms of individual rights together with the agreed standards (laws) of society. At a later stage all morality may be seen as a matter of universal principles, which can stand in judgement over society itself.

These changes in moral thinking and the grounds of moral justification constitute an important aspect of the interpersonal dimension of faith.

(D) Social awareness

'When I was a child my family was my world, but now . . .'

Faith is usually a shared activity. We do our faithing *together,* in union with those to whom we feel we belong. Part of the way of faith is the way in which, and the extent to which, we draw the boundaries around *our* community of faith. As we develop we get different answers when we ask ourselves the question that the lawyer asked Jesus: 'Who is my neighbour?'[15] To begin with, the family is everything. It constitutes our 'Church'. From this centre we later expand to embrace an increasingly wide constituency. It is composed initially of 'those like us', then of those with whom we have anything to do or who share our world-view at least to some extent. Finally, perhaps, it comes to comprise the whole human race.

Fowler refers to the way that ecumenism is viewed differently by adults at different stages, from a 'some-of-my-best-friends-are-Catholics' sort of ecumenism, through a 'let's-sort-out-our-doctrinal-differences-and-agreements' ecumenism, to an 'I-am-open-to-being-converted-to-your-truth' ecumenism. If meaning-making is something we do together, then how one sees and determines who 'we' are is a very important part of the way of faith.

(E) Relation to authority

'When I was a child the big people told me what to do, but now . . .'

Well, to be honest, for most of us it's not that different now! Social psychologists inform us that tall people are still more likely to be promoted. They are 'looked up to' psychologically as well as literally. As we form and find faith together, other people's faith is a potent influence on our own. In science, history and geography—as well as in religion, politics and ethics—what 'they say' is often very important to us. But the group who make up the 'they' changes as we develop.

Who are my authorities for truth and meaning? How do I rely on their authority in forming my own view of reality? Our earliest authority figures are the adults on whom we are dependent. Later the class is represented by valued groups and individuals, whether peer groups of teenage friends or business colleagues, or our church and its ministers. Later still we may recognize as authorities more distant people who share our ideals. Finally we may take note of a wide diversity of authorities to whom we are open, sometimes despite disagreements. The boundaries of this group change because I am drawing them differently, as I revise my way of treating people as authorities for my life. This aspect of faith thus 'describes the way persons at each stage interpret and rely upon sources of authoritative insight or "truth" regarding the nature of the ultimate environment' (*LM* 40).

This strand of faith—along with our social perspective-taking, our way of forming the boundaries of our social awareness, and our style of moral thinking—determines our interpersonal relationships in family, school, work and church. Together they constitute the horizontal dimension of our faithing. But they also affect, and are affected by, its vertical dimension: our interpretation of and relationship with what we believe to be ultimate. The final two aspects of faith (world-view formation and interpretation of symbols) articulate what most people most readily recognize as 'faith'. They seem to be the aspects that are most clearly relevant to the concerns of Christian nurture. For it is these two strands of faithing that determine how we construct our ultimate environment, through and with the symbols of faith.

(F) Forming a world-view

'When I was a child I took everything for granted, but now . . .'

Fowler calls this aspect the 'form of world coherence'. It is the way in which we create—discover our ultimate environment as a unified whole, a *world*-view. It is our way of unifying our experience, of 'holding it all together', of creating one story by which to live.

One of the great sea-changes in our lives comes—if it comes at all— when the implicit, tacit, unconscious processes which do all this work for us are gradually and painfully replaced by a self-conscious, explicit

13

system of meaning. We may have the same world-view as before, the difference lies in the way we possess it. Like inherited property its nature remains what it was, but it *is* different. Now it belongs to me.

At this point we change from receiving a world-view that is provided by other people, wrapped around us like someone else's hand-me-down overcoat, to choosing deliberately (as it seems), or designing and making, our own clothes of meaning.[16] Between these two stages, as we shall see, comes a time of vulnerable nakedness. Fowler's research shows that some adults may later move even beyond this stage of choosing their own overcoat to a new vulnerability where the clothes they thought were 'just us' no longer quite fit. Now the comfortable shoes begin to pinch, and the dress on which we have spent a fortune—or a fortnight—no longer satisfies. If the metaphor can stand the strain, we might now talk of our need for a new set of clothes: clothes with more room in them, clothes that are made for all seasons, clothes that have more give to them—clothes, perhaps, with holes in them? (Possibly the metaphor—or the material—won't stretch *that* far!)

We do speak of people's faith becoming more 'open', 'flexible' or 'inclusive' as they mature: not less vigorous or committed, but less restrictive and narrow. Those who minister to young people and students rejoice in their enthusiastic faith, their idealistic certainties, their fervent but sometimes rather too closed Christianity (whether it be evangelical, anglo-catholic, charismatic or liberal). The young can be so sure of themselves. But we know that they will learn![17] When we see them again at 25 or 35 (or 65) they will have changed in many ways. Very often their faith will have changed with them. It will still be fervent, perhaps, and its content *may* still be largely what it was at 19. But, even so, its form is likely to have changed. In all probability it will be more open to and inclusive of other viewpoints; more sensitive to the messiness of life and the complexity of truth; more 'balanced'. They will have changed—and so shall we. At different times we hold things together differently. For everything there is a season. This is a central aspect of our activity of faith.

(G) Relation to symbols

'When I was a child everything was like magic, but now . . .'

We come finally to the role of symbols in our faith: how we respond to them and how we use them, and the developing 'sequence of levels in symbolic competence' (*LM* 41).

There is no faith without symbols, whether we think of the symbolic actions and objects of worship and Church life, or the symbol-stories and picture language that inform our lives (e.g. our images of what *we* are and will become, or our picture of the *universe* as a desert, an intricate machine or a gift from a friend). Young children relish symbols. To look in on an infant assembly as they light the Advent candle or listen for Father Christmas's sleigh bells is a revelation to many adults. Awe and wonder are natural to little children. For them symbols are magical.[18] It is only later, when children become so concrete in their thinking, that symbols begin to lose that magic as they treat (mistreat) them literally. At one stage we cannot speak of the hand of God without wondering if he cuts his nails (but not yet, perhaps, whether 'he' is the right pronoun). Even when we begin to think abstractly the power of symbols is not wholly restored. At one stage at least we have to translate, explain and unpack their meaning before we can allow them to speak to us. So baptism services must be prefaced by explanations of what the water and the dipping really mean; and confirmation and marriage preparation courses strive to expound the real meaning of drinking from chalices and exchanging rings. Later, for some at least, this 'demythologizing' of symbols becomes redundant.

These individuals have recaptured something of the direct power that symbols had for them in early childhood. This stage is not entered into, however, unless the stage of explanation has first been traversed. When it comes it may involve a more sophisticated ability to hold together a range of different meanings in the understanding of one symbol.

These then are Fowler's 'windows into faith': the multiple aspects or facets or strands that together constitute the way of faithing. It is these aspects that change as faith develops, and it is to this theory of faith development that we must now turn.

2

When is Faith?

CHANGES AND STAGES

When we talk about faith as content, we know that it can change. 'When I was a child I thought of God as someone sitting on a cloud with a long white beard, but now . . .' But in this book we are thinking of faith as the *way* of faith: the way in which we image, relate to, understand and believe in this content. And it is James Fowler's claim that this way (these ways) also change: that the processes, structures and forms of faith *develop* through various *stages* of faith (or 'stage like styles', cf. *MSDF* 141, 143).

The idea of stage development is found in more than one type of psychology and it does not always mean the same thing. Erik Erikson, for example, has described a sequence of eight stages across the human life-cycle.[1] At each there is a 'crisis' brought about by significant biological changes accompanied by emotional and cognitive changes. We cannot evade the passage of years which forces us to face up to adolescence, middle age and old age with whatever resources are available to us at the time. The exposition of these stages, the crises and their resolution belong to *neo-Freudian psychology*. Fowler acknowledges his debt to Erikson's ideas.

A quite different conception of stage is to be found in the developmental accounts of the other psychologists who figure importantly in Fowler's scheme. The initiator here is Piaget. In his theory of the construction of intelligence the characterizing feature is the interaction between ourselves and our environment, with development dependent upon what we can make of the experience in which we are involved, and the degree to which such experiences promote alterations. Development here is only partly age-related. We can, so to speak, have a 'young' head on old shoulders. The focus in this approach is on the structures or patterns of cognition (thinking and knowing). This cognitive structural approach, or *cognitive developmental psychology,* has been utilized by Robert Selman in his study of social perspective, and by Lawrence Kohlberg in his study of moral reasoning.

What Fowler seems to have done is to combine Erikson's view of development over a lifespan with other sequences of development— Fowler's own aspects, facets or dimensions of faith. He has set out the sequences of development in logical reasoning, social perspective and moral reasoning and aligned them with developmental sequences in four other 'dimensions'. As we have seen these four are a person's bounds of social awareness, her locus of authority, form of world coherence and symbolic functioning.

Just as Piaget discerned stages in the way we think, and Kohlberg proposed stages of moral judgement, so Fowler claims to have discovered six stages or styles of faith. The claim is a big one. These stages are regarded as *universal* at least in principle, that is they are the stages that in principle everyone might pass through although most of us don't get very far (and in some cultures some stages are unlikely to be reached). They are claimed to be *invariant* (we cannot 'skip' a stage) and *hierarchical* (each stage follows on from the last: incorporating, modifying and augmenting its processes).

The idea of the stage as a 'structural whole', 'an integrated system of operations (structures) of thought and valuing' (*FSM* 74) which creates, relates to and knows a person's ultimate environment, has been the subject of some criticism. The notion of the stage is not nowadays as firm a part of cognitive development theory as it used to be. This is to some extent because of the difficulty in establishing the relations between several components when development, and so transition, is going on all the time. It is now recognized that, for practical purposes, the most useful information is the *order* in which developmental features appear. This should be borne in mind as we survey Fowler's work. Fowler's stage descriptions should not be taken for portrait photographs of a 'still life' but rather as impressionistic paintings of a subject in motion.[2]

STAGES OF FAITH

It is worth commenting that Fowler's stages of relative stability (or 'equilibration') alternate with equally important periods of transition when the aspects of a person's faith are shifting from one mode to another. These transitions often occur 'when the equilibrium of a given stage is upset by encounters with crises, novelties, and experiences of disclosure and challenge, which threaten the limits of the person's present patterns' (*FSM* 67). In the sample of 359 children and adults

17

whose interviews are reported in *Stages of Faith,* over 30% were regarded by Fowler and his associates as 'transitional' (*SF* 318). At these times in people's lives they are restructuring their faith, losing the old way of being in faith preparatory to developing another faith style, and thereby perhaps suffering the death of one (way of viewing) God prior to the resurrection of another. Some of these transitions can take from five to seven years (*N* 7).

As we shall see in Chapter 3, Fowler's account and his research methods have their limitations. His 'grand hypothesis' of faith development is something that he himself often presents quite tentatively. But it remains the case that very many people acknowledge *some truth* in what he says. Very often they recognize themselves and other people they know in these pictures of faith. Sometimes they feel compelled to admit that such pictures do fit together like the frames of a film, so as to produce a moving picture which can illustrate their own life stories or the journeys of faith of others. Despite the reservations, then, Fowler's faith development story deserves retelling. We are convinced that it will chime in with many people's own experience.

In giving our account of the so-called 'Stages of Faith' we shall begin with the diagrammatic illustrations which Fowler frequently uses as illuminating ideograms. We have been bold enough—or, perhaps, foolish enough—to attempt a retitling of the stages. We do this in some trepidation, knowing both that Fowler has always been wary of 'premature popularization' and that his own titles have been carefully chosen to summarize the key elements of the stages. But they *are* a mouthful (especially for British readers!) and we have dared to offer our own, but always adding Fowler's titles in square brackets.

It should be noted that the developments seen here represent *both* a development in a person's faithing *and* a development of that person's self. Faith development and ego development go together. In this area of the evolution of the self Fowler draws on the work of Robert Kegan.[3] In his more recent writings (e.g. *FDPC*) Fowler adds titles from Kegan's work to his faith stages. We have included these within the same square brackets, separated from Fowler's own title by a slash (/).

Fowler's research is based on structured, semi-clinical interviews of from one to three hours each with over 500 individuals. The original Research Interview and its analysis, together with details of the sample, are given in the Appendices to *Stages of Faith.* Much fuller details of the later Research Interview are given in the *Manual*. Some critical comments on the research method are detailed below (pp 47f). Although we shall sometimes refer to 'Stage 2 people' or a 'Stage 5 person', strictly speaking it is their responses—and the ways of thinking, relating, etc. that they imply—which are at that particular stage.

FOWLER'S STAGES OF FAITH

Stage 0: 'Nursed Faith' or 'Foundation Faith' [Primal Faith/The Incorporative Self]

Age: 0-4 approximately.
This is not so much a stage as a 'pre-stage', which is not really open to empirical investigation. (Fowler has no interviews with one-year-olds to confirm his account here!)

As the diagram shows, our faithing begins in the context of being picked up and nursed. For the child in her mother's arms, the 'ultimate environment' is constituted by face, breasts, cot and rattle. Parents are so important because they form and constitute the infant's world. Here faith begins with a disposition to trust. As Erikson has argued, in the first years of a child's life the struggle of trust with the temptation to mistrust is crucial to the development of the character-strength of hope, and lies at the basis of all future religious faith.[4]

Kegan describes selfhood at this stage in terms of the 'incorporative self': a description that is true insofar as the infant is his experiences and only slowly separates himself from his mother and the rest of the 'outside world' (but see Chapter 1, note 13).

Clearly the nursing, 'mothering' care of the young child is a real and vital part of any sort of nurture that we might dare to call 'Christian'. It gives us, Fowler insists, 'our first *pre-images* of God' mediated through 'recognizing eyes and confirming smiles' (*SF* 121). As a counterweight to more intellectual notions of Christian nurture, we should note that the word appears to come from the Latin *nutrire,* meaning 'to suckle or nourish'. We are loved into knowing and feeling, as we are loved into being.

Stage 1: 'Chaotic Faith' or 'Unordered Faith' or 'Impressionistic Faith'
[Intuitive–Projective Faith/The Impulsive Self]

Age: 3/4-7/8 approximately.

This is the stage at which the child's relatively uncontrolled imagination yields a chaos of powerful images. The child's limited ability to think prevents her creating order out of this chaos. As the diagram shows, her 'ultimate environment' is composed of a cloud made up of a collage of images and beliefs derived from her own imagination, from stories told her by other people, and from her first experiences of  the outside world. It has discrete boundaries from which she doesn't escape. Her world is created by projecting these images on to its boundary, as in a well-known science-fiction story where a high-tech machine for keeping the kids quiet projected images from their imagination on to the walls and ceilings of their nursery. In the story the images (of African lions) finally devour the children. At Stage 1 most children feel as if they might. In a world where real and fantasy objects exist side by side, the child may expect at any moment to see a lion around the corner, Father Christmas up the chimney, or Jesus peering at him from the dark corner of his room. Thinking is more likely to be 'intuitive' (immediate, unreasoned) than discursive ('rational', 'logical'). 'Reasoning with young children' is a brave enterprise indeed!

It is at this stage that the child's world is made up of images more than stories. Her world is 'episodic' and 'impressionistic'. It consists of one thing after another. It is not patterned like a narrative. The world is a montage or scrap-book, not yet ordered by an appreciation of the laws of cause and effect or the conservation of matter. The egocentric child—who *is* its impulses (*FDPC* 60—the child as 'the impulsive self')—lacks the ability to adopt another's perspective. Moral ('premoral'?) judgments are based on the child's observations of rewards and punishments and make no reference to intention. Social awareness is limited to the family. Authority figures are big adults.

At this stage faithing, like everything else, is essentially an imitation of what the child can pick up from adults. Parents know the joys and the difficulties of this era, as the child learns the possibilities and limits of being itself. Dependable, structured parenting is crucial here. Equally crucial is the provision of appropriate images on which the child can feed. Symbols are viewed magically; they are what they represent. The powerful symbols of Christian liturgy and Christian belonging will contribute deep and lasting images in this stage of faith. Young children who are excluded from ritual and sacrament 'because they don't yet understand' may be being cut off from a vital form of nourishment. It is interesting that very young children, while they may picture God using imagery that is anthropomorphic (i.e. picturing the divine in human form as 'Big Daddy in the sky'), are more likely at this stage to use non-anthropomorphic images like 'air' or 'sun'. It is at the next faith stage that the standard, over-literal 'pictures of God' are produced.

Stage 2: 'Ordering Faith'
[Mythic-Literal Faith/The Imperial Self]

Age: 6/7—11/12 approximately, and some adults. At this stage the child develops real skills of thinking. The chaos of his world-view at Stage 1 is now slowly being sorted out. His power to think, to unify experience, to trace the pattern of cause and effect, and to know a story when he hears one, enables the junior-school child to order his experience. Hence the diagram: the chaotic, fantasy-world is still part of his universe, but it is now coming under his control and can be limited in its scope to the world of play and fiction. 'Is this a *true* story?', the child now wants to know. The world is becoming predictable, and losing its enchantment. In the picture, therefore, on the other side of this young thinker lies ordered, structured, 'linear reality': the fact he has separated from fiction, 'objective knowledge' distinct from private fantasy.

This is the great era of story. A parent who takes her children of six and eight to an adventure film must expect two very different responses. For the younger child the film is a chaos of images, a collage of episodes swept up as it were from the cutting-room floor. He will not be able to tell 'the story' of the film. But the older child can and will—with gusto and at enormous length! Story-telling is important at this stage as providing 'a central way of establishing identity, through

21

the learning of the stories of those groups and communities to which one belongs' (*FDPC* 61). This is a very important feature of this type of faithing for the Christian educator. 'Telling our story' is a major part of what is involved in Christian religious education. But there are dangers here, too, for the child who is not yet capable of abstract reflection, nor of self-critically pulling herself out of the story and assessing it. Perhaps this is why stories go down so well in assemblies and church groups—*until* the story-teller attempts to add 'the moral'! At this stage children can only tell stories in life, not about life. We shall have to wait a while, until she moves to a further stage, before we shall be able to hear from her any brief and succinct summary of the movie of life.

Being now able to take the perspective of others in a simple and concrete way (at least those others who are like themselves), the child can imagine what it is like to be a character in a story. But she has 'little real notion of the interiority of the other' (*M* 83). This is a potent time for prejudices to be formed through stories. If people are to develop beyond this stage, the master-stories on offer must be open-ended enough to allow a future escape.

It is not just the stories from which people at this stage may need later to escape (and Stage 2 people, we should note, include a couple of teenagers and adults in their twenties and fifties in Fowler's sample). At Stage 2 symbols are treated in a rather wooden, one-dimensional and literal way. Like everything else, they are limited by the form of thinking of this stage, which is intrinsically concrete. God is often seen—through the child's ability to construct 'God's perspective'—in anthropomorphic terms, as a stern, just parent. As some of the reactions to the controversial Bishops of Woolwich (in the 1960s) and Durham (in our day) have revealed, such an image of God—created by the way of faith of a junior-aged child, and proper and appropriate at that stage—may stay on into adulthood. Similarly Stage 2 moral thinking (which now finds a place for considerations of motive) is largely based on an ethic of reciprocal fairness and immanent justice: 'you scratch my back and I'll scratch yours'. This is an ethic which may later need to be transcended.

'Mark' is a ten-year-old; he responded to the interviewer in this way:

> *Interviewer: Now, you were telling me earlier your thoughts about heaven, can you tell me those again?*

Mark: Well, I just think of heaven as a place where there is no evil being done and every animal's home is safe, no blood sports, which I don't like. I don't know whether everyone would be vegetarian or not, I'm not quite sure. God would become the king, and all that, and all the people that (I don't believe in hell)—I think that all the people that have done wrong would either, wouldn't get to heaven, or would, well, wouldn't be treated as well in heaven.

Interviewer: Right. And God would be . . .

Mark: Well, God would be on this massive throne, with Jesus at his right hand. He wouldn't be really rich, he'd just be, have equality.

Interviewer: And what would that mean?

Mark: Well he'd be able to tell people what to do even though they . . . just he would be like a king except he wouldn't do anything wrong. He'd make the right decisions not the wrong decisions and there wouldn't be any government.

Interviewer: There wouldn't? What would there be instead?

Mark: Well they wouldn't need one, because everyone would do the right thing (laughs) and there would be no prisons or anything like that.

Kegan calls this the age of the 'imperial self', for the self is now constituted by its needs and interests. Now the child is (not her impulses, but) her needs and wishes. She cannot yet reflect on or examine herself. Loving restraint and support is needed at this stage if the child is to move without too much trauma into a more reflective mode of being. If adults remain in this stage great patience will be required of their friends and ministers.

Parents and teachers will not need reminding that the junior-aged child is intensely 'club-able', in the sense of wanting to join in most things (and sometimes in another sense also!). The junior child is one who belongs, and whose self-image is partly constituted by such belonging as his or her social horizon widens ('I am a member of the choir'; 'of Miss Smith's class'; 'of the Cubs'; 'of the Girls' Brigade'). Churches are often intensely 'successful' with children at this age, if success is measured by such affiliative activity. When the same people drift away in early adolescence it is partly at least because *simple belonging* no longer contributes so much to their sense of identity. At the next faith stage the self is constituted by its relationships and its roles, it is made up by its significant social ties. At Stage 3 interpersonal *relationships* are everything.

Stage 3: 'Conforming Faith'
[Synthetic-Conventional Faith/The Interpersonal Self]

'Greg' is a twenty-one-year-old college student and keen sportsman. He shows his reliance on interpersonal relationships in this interview in the way he describes what can be called his 'embeddedness' in the group with which he plays basketball:

> . . . I've always given up something for Lent, and one of the last things to go from this college I suppose would be alcohol, and so every, well since I've been here, I've given up alcohol for Lent . . . It renders me liable for ridicule because as I'm a member of a basketball team there's a certain association with drink after matches, fines and things, and so I suppose it was a test of my faith to turn around to those twenty-odd guys and say: 'Look, I'm not drinking alcohol for the next six weeks because I'm a Christian and it's the season of Lent . . .' I was expecting to get a lot of stick for it off them, but the captain turned around and said: 'Right, that's fine, you're still going to be drinking the fines but you can have non-alcoholic drinks', and so in a way they accepted me as I was, and I was really happy about that.

Age: 11/12-17/18 approximately, and many adults.
The shift to Stage 3 is marked by a revolution in the way that a person's faithing is done. Now the adolescent or adult develops the ability to think abstractly and reflectively, and there is a new capacity for perspective-taking—and a related excitement in interpersonal relationships. Fowler puts it like this:

> I see you seeing me:
> I see the me I think you see . . .
> You see you according to me:
> You see the you you think I see. (*FDPC* 64)

This new self-awareness and reflective ability leads to a new awareness of what I am in relation to other people. Now 'I *am* my relationships, I *am* my roles' (*FDPC* 66), and I feel a deep desire to conform to the expectations of these newly-significant 'others' in my life, who are sometimes reconstructed by me into a 'generalized other'. This is the great *conforming* period of my life as far as my self-image and my faith are concerned. It is pictured above with the self standing within a circle of others with whom it has a face-to-face relationship—peers, parents, teachers, church leaders, or mentors of some other description. What 'they say' is now very important to me, and my faith is largely formed by their influence. This aspect of the stage has been described as 'the tyranny of the "they"'.[5] I arrange them around myself and try to weld together a bits-and-pieces faith from their influences and their perceptions of me, despite the diverse values and beliefs that they express. This produces an 'heteronomous' (other-dependent) faith, contributed by the overlapping theatres of influence of those whom I respect.

My social awareness is dominated by this (my) 'in-group'. They are my chosen authority figures. The ancient psychological and philosophical problem of the Many and the One is reflected here in my attempt to pull together and hold together this very disparate collection of faith influences, which otherwise would naturally fly apart. I do succeed, at this stage, in 'keeping it all together'. But my meaning-making synthesis is not yet something I can reflect upon. It is a system or world-view that I have built tacitly, without a full consciousness of what I was about. 'In this stage one is *embedded* in his or her faith outlook' (*CA* 184). My beliefs and values are, in consequence, often themselves hidden from me. I don't really know what I really believe.

Nevertheless I am quite able and willing to think about myself and the stories of my faith. Those of us who are at this stage can compose a fairly comprehensive story of our past: 'the story of our stories' (*SF* 152). But we remain unable to reflect much on our ideology. Faith is here being synthesized, not analyzed. 'Synthetic' in Fowler's title for this stage does not imply artificial, only 'built-up'—'pulling together and drawing disparate elements into a unity, a synthesis' (*CA* 183). Symbols and rituals are not things I can separate from the things they symbolize. Fowler quotes George Santayana, 'We cannot know who first discovered water. But we can be sure that it was not the fish' (*SF* 161, cf. 177). At Stage 3 I am like a fish immersed in a watery medium, unable to leap out and look down on the water. I hardly know how (or that) I am in faith, or where my faith comes from. It is a time of going with a particular faith-current, or faith-crowd. There is no place for the individualistic 'knight of faith' here, swimming against the tide.

Stage 3 moral thinking is represented either by a 'living up to expectations' or a 'law and order' morality. Images of God are 'no longer physically anthropomorphic, but are based on "personal" qualities of the deity'—such as friend, comforter or guide (*LM* 64).

25

People at this faith stage provide very exciting opportunities for the Christian educator. They are capable of reasoning in a new and more powerful way, and are much more able to cope with arguments and discussion about theology. A more sophisticated account of religion can now be given and appreciated. Many teachers regard this as the time when education in religion can begin seriously.

Yet it can also be a difficult time for the Christian educator. It is true that adolescents are beginning to think abstractly, and therefore more appropriately as far as some aspects of religion are concerned. But they have not yet started to think *for themselves.* It is always difficult to converse with people in a certain place if they do not know why they are there, or even that they are there. Tacit meaning-making is blind to itself. It is like the tacit knowledge we have that enables us to recognize other people's faces or to ride a bicycle. It is knowledge that can only become explicit and subject to critical scrutiny by becoming something else (explicit knowledge).[6] The parent or teacher of adolescents needs to recognize that at the moment many of them simply cannot see where their values and beliefs come from, or how they have created their world-views. At this stage getting them to concentrate on how they are doing the riding may only result in their falling off the bike altogether. Sometimes our ideologies can *only* 'operate not in front of our eyes but from behind our backs'.[7]

But for many people this is not their final stage. Ahead lies new and difficult terrain for the pilgrim on the life journey of faith. Stage 3 is a sort of juggling act. It can be a bit of a strain. I have to stand in the midst of all those others with their differing understandings and expectations of *me* (and their different beliefs and values, although I hardly notice them at this stage). At Stage 3 I struggle to keep all these 'significant others' up in the air together through my faith juggling, or (to change the image) to hold their influences on me together in tension despite the differences which force them apart. Many people cannot keep this up for ever. The juggler misses his catch. The ropes break.

There are all these others with whom I am in relationship: teachers, youth-leaders, friends, workmates. Eventually I may begin to wonder: 'Who am I when I am *not* in relationship with this circle of people around me?' This question became acute for one teenager who was interviewed by David Day and Philip May for their valuable study, *Teenage Beliefs.* Her use of the word 'faith' may not be Fowler's, but the extract is worth quoting:

Barbara . . . was greatly challenged not long after becoming a Christian by the loss of her two closest friends who both left the area:

'*I found that really hard, 'cos I depended on them an awful lot for support and friendship. So when they left, I really had to realize where I stood and whether it was faith—whether I was relying on God or them. That was a big step, 'cos I really had to grow as a person, and become strong.*'[8]

Not everyone leaves the stage of conforming faith, there is a form of Stage 3 in which a fair number of adults find equilibrium. But for those who do go on to Stage 4 this situation cannot be sustained. . . .

Stage 4: 'Choosing Faith' or 'Either/Or Faith'
[Individuative-Reflective Faith/The Institutional Self]

Age: from approximately 17/18 onwards, or from the 30s or 40s onwards.
Now I can no longer tolerate the diversity of roles to which Stage 3 faithing commits me. And I can no longer tolerate having my faith at second-hand. I must now know

who I am for myself, when I am not being defined by my relationships with other people. And I must do my own thing as far as faith is concerned. I must make my *own* meaning and create my own world. I must choose and own a faith for myself.

Now I have leapt out of the water. I can look down on relationships and my previously implicit system of beliefs and values. In a peculiar way I can even look down on myself. I can stand somewhere (partly) outside of myself and critically reflect on what and how I believe. We have heard much in recent years of 'out of the body' experiences. This is a sort of 'out of culture' and 'out of myself' experience. To put it differently, instead of being simply wrapped up in my faith I have begun to be able to hold it at arm's length and see it from a different perspective. This is a more critical, reflective way of thinking and a new ('third person') skill of perspective-taking. This is 'critical distancing from one's previous . . . value system' (*SF* 179). I have begun to take charge of myself: my commitments and evaluations, my beliefs and relationships. I have developed an 'executive ego' (Fowler), an 'institutional self' (Kegan).

At Stage 4 one is willing and able to judge oneself in the light of the outlook of others, but the impulse to justify one's own truth may result in the creation of caricatures of the faith of other people. Morality is now increasingly a matter of judging on the basis of moral principles, particularly the ideal of justice, although class or group bias restricts this.

The diagram shows me outside the Stage 3 circle(s) of conventional faith—observing them, deciding between them, choosing a world-view. My system-building is now an explicit process. I know what I am about. My faith is 'autonomous' (self-directed). I now treat as authorities those who agree with *me*: I have internalized authority. I am really conscious for the first time of social systems and institutions with their own perspectives and their range of faith options, of a variety of beliefs and values. Despite the 'vertigo of relativity' that I feel at this panorama of pluralism, I know that I cannot shirk my responsibility to decide for myself what is right. I now choose, or at least feel that I am choosing, my authorities and my gods, my ideology and world-view. Previously I was rather blind to the significance of my beliefs and those of others, a sort of 'blind juggler' who did not really know what he was juggling with. Now I see. 'What were previously tacit and unexamined convictions and beliefs must now become matters of more explicit commitment and accountability' (*BABC* 62).

Everything is now up for grabs and open to examination. 'Truth must "fit" with other elements of one's outlook taken as a whole' (*LM* 72). Stage 4 should be seen as an effective, emotional stance as much as it is an intellectual one. Yet it shares many of the strengths and weaknesses of the employment of critical reason in human psychology and the history of ideas. Thus there is the danger of a self which 'over-assimilates "reality" and the perspectives of others into its own world-view' (*SF* 183). There is the danger of an arid over-intellectualism, which shows itself in the fervent 'explanation' and 'demythologizing' of symbols and stories. 'But what does it *mean*?', I am forever asking (*SF* 180). There is the danger of a conceited autonomy and pretended independence. Loose of mother's apron strings I may forget where I came from; and forget too those who had so much to do with forming my 'self-chosen' values, and on whom I still rely. Seeking a perspective 'above' myself and others I may pretend that I can jump out of my own skin or exist out of all cultural waters.

In some ways the worst danger is the over-simplifying naiveness and 'either/or' quality that often marks this new, 'self-determined' faith. I want such a tidy faith. I am so determined to button up my faith-overcoat. I am now so conscious of my own responsibility for my faith and its coherence that I will tend to collapse paradoxes and tensions. Those who have lived through this stage and moved to a different form of faith may look back and argue that the tension is sometimes one that cannot be dealt with in this way. It has to be lived with, rather than resolved, they will claim. We may here revive our earlier image of forces held together, but here they are forces within rather than outside the self and its belief system. The strain of forces pulling in opposite directions can seem intolerable and unnecessary; but in the tent of meaning, cutting one set of guy ropes eases the tension in the canvas only by collapsing the entire structure. But this is to anticipate. . . .

Fowler regards the move to this stage of faith—the Stage 3/4 transition—as one of the most significant in the development of faith. It is a long transition and it can be very traumatic. It often comes when a person 'leaves home'—not just, or even at all, geographically but *emotionally.* We must expect it, then, in college students or the newly-wed; in those who start work for the first time or who find new influences in their lives which are part of a social horizon that is wider than parents, friends, school and church. We shall find it in those who have changed homes or jobs or partners; in those whose parents have died or who have retired or have been made redundant. It sometimes leads to an individualistic or group-related atheism or agnosticism, but it may equally result in a self-selected and consciously chosen commitment to a religious faith community. It is a profoundly significant time for Christian education: a time of becoming oneself; of taking responsibility for one's faith; of owning one's world-view, one's life style and one's Church (N 3). Christian educators need to be sensitive and responsive to the possibilities—and the problems—of this faith stage transition. Above all, they need to give such a person space to make her own moves, to do her own learning, and to find her own vocation.

This is all part of growing up, even if it does not take place until we are 90. And growing up in faith always involves a loss of (an old) faith, and a time out in the wilderness before the new way of faith can be entered upon. Growing up in faith, if Fowler's stages and transitions have any truth in them, will include a painful growing out of one faith, preparatory to our growing into another.

'Sarah' is a forty-year-old mother of three. She described in her interview how her 'image of God' had changed over the years (and also, in passing, gives a charming anecdote about her five-year-old son's image of God). Most of her interview showed Stage 4 characteristics:

> Sarah: . . . images have changed from the man in the clouds which you've all got when you're small, because you have to pick up a physical picture, so now I find thinking of Jesus as a man very difficult, whereas I can think of God as a presence, a spiritual presence I think, but it's almost like a blanket that'll come round . . . it is just a presence, but I can feel that presence sometimes; if I want to I can snuggle back in it, in that presence, so it's gone from the fatherly figure, I think, all the way to that, and it will no doubt change again. . . .
>
> Interviewer: Right. How do you see it changing?
>
> Sarah: Well, I guess it will because I need that feeling of what God is now as a comforting sort of cuddly presence . . . but I guess maybe perhaps when you're older you need something else. . . . My little one on one occasion went to school with his hand up in the air. He was holding my hand on one side and his hand up in the air like that, and I said 'What are you doing?' and he said 'I'm going to school with God this morning and he's holding my hand.' . . . I haven't ever been like that, but I mean that's what he needed, that was his vision at that time. . . .

Stage 5: 'Balanced Faith' or 'Inclusive Faith' or 'Both/And Faith' [9]
[Conjunctive Faith/The Inter-Individual Self]

Age: rare before 30.
Some 7% of Fowler's sample show characteristics of another, different stage. There is some evidence that those who have been disadvantaged or who have suffered in some way enter this stage earlier than others. Fowler writes, 'unusual before mid-life, Stage 5 knows the sacrament of defeat and the reality of irrevocable commitments and

acts' (*FSM* 73). He is referring here to the changes that come upon people as they learn through coping with failure and living with the consequences of their earlier decisions.

At Stage 5 the unity, coherence and tidiness of Stage 4 begins to fade. The glue comes unstuck here and there; the seams come unstitched. There is a new openness in this style of faith. Fowler regards it as a *reworking* of our Stage 4 faith. 'What the previous stage struggled to bring under consciousness and control, the present stage must allow to become porous and permeable' (*FDF* 30). Fowler's diagram for this stage is less easy to interpret than some of the previous ones. Apparently it shows a person's faith-formed world-view (the triangle) inter-penetrated by the circles of other interpretations. At this stage we come to respect the truth in the viewpoints of others. We are more capable now of keeping in tension the paradoxes and polarities of faith and life,[10] and of living with ambiguity—and even apparent irration-ality—in the meaning-system we have created for ourselves. This is made possible by a new style of thinking, which Fowler calls 'dialectical' or 'dialogical' knowing. With this we can see many sides of an issue at the same time. It is like the mutual speaking and hearing of a conversation, in this case a 'conversation' between the knower and the known (*SF* 185). Truth, we now believe, is no either/or thing, but 'must be approached from at least two or more angles of vision simultaneously' (*BABC* 65). We remain committed to our truth tradition, but cease to force the pattern of Reality into our own framework of thought. Fowler writes:

> The person of Stage 5 makes her or his own experience of truth the principle by which other claims to truth are tested. But he or she assumes that each genuine perspective will augment and correct aspects of the other. . . . (*SF* 187)

This faith stance is one that is hard to describe, but its consequences are easy to discern and well-captured in the metaphor of 'balance'. Someone who is at Stage 5 lives with, internalizes, includes and keeps in balance multiple perspectives on reality. Such a person is truly, but discriminatingly, open to other people. At this stage we can dwell within and affirm our group's deepest meanings, while 'simultaneously recognizing that they are relative, partial and inevitably distorting apprehensions' of Reality (*SF* 198). A Stage 5 person shows real empathy with others, and a true openness to their insights into truth and value—even when those others belong to very different traditions. She 'seeks understanding rather than explanation', and is less interested than she was in defending her own world-view (*M* 153). This openness extends to the symbols of faith also, which at this stage regain their

31

evocative power as their interpreter is ('postcritically') freed from the compulsion to translate and explain them.

The openness to others and to the complexities of Reality is expressed in a new humility in a person's faith-knowing. It is also evidenced in a new recognition of our interdependent existence, very different from the independent knowing and relating of Stage 4 (*my* faith). The form of moral judgement also changes, so that it is marked by a recognition of universal principles which transcend particular individual or social perspectives. 'Stage 5 is ready for a community identification beyond tribal, racial, class, or ideological boundaries' (*LM* 82).

The self is still in the picture, and its well-being is important to it. But the transcendent call of duty is beginning to be heard and the self has started to know what it is truly to give to others. It is more and more willing to suspend its own views 'in an effort to feel and grasp the full impact of others' experiences' (*LM* 81). Through the open pores of this style of faith, the self is beginning to leak out for others. Fowler writes:

> With the seriousness that can arise when life is more than half over, this stage is ready to spend and be spent for the cause of conserving and cultivating the possibility of others, generating identity and meaning. (*SF* 198)

Christian educators need to recognize the features of this stage in which the learner is more complex, balanced, inclusive and open in her faithing. Too often the Church fears Stage 5 learners because they are difficult to control, pigeon-hole or understand. Whatever the content of their faith life, their attitude will appear rather too liberal and all-embracing for some. The many-sided approach of balanced or inclusive faith can be very wearing for a Christian education approach that is more used to straight-line argumentation and a narrow focus of concerns and ideas. Stage 5 is 'both/and', and that is often more difficult to cope with and control than the 'either/or' perspective of Stage 4. At Stage 5 there is also a new willingness to let symbol, myth and story speak to us again. 'Having looked critically at traditions and translated their meanings into conceptual understandings . . . we learn again to let symbols have the initiative with us' (*N* 3). The Bible narrative can once again 'read our lives, reforming and reshaping' (*N* 4). Christian education at Stage 5 must allow for this feature as well.

These changes only come with time, a factor that points up the significance of inter-generational relationships and activities.

Grandparents can often understand and cope with adolescents in ways that the teenagers' own parents (and Granny herself when she was 40!) cannot. The balanced faith stage (station?) is further on down the railway line. From there a perspective can sometimes be achieved that can find more value in earlier parts of the journey, more value perhaps than a less remote viewpoint would recognize. This is not quite an eternal perspective, a view *sub specie aeternitatis,* but there is at this stage an ability to transcend the problems and concerns of the particular. This new detachment and sense of perspective can be pastorally most helpful for those who are inevitably 'up to their necks' in their particular current lives.

> *Sally: I find increasingly the symbolism of openness is very important as Christians and, um, whether that means open to outsiders. . . . We are trying to believe as Christians. Christ has told us to exist for the people outside, not just say, 'you're born a Jew', 'you are a Jew', 'you are not a Jew'. 'I am a Jew, but I follow Christ', 'I am a Christian, I want you to come here and see what Christ has to offer you', or 'I want to love you', or 'I want to offer you whatever it is you need' . . . I think if you let go of the thing that you're trying to place around yourself so that you can say 'that's my faith', 'that's what I believe', 'that's what the Bible says', 'that's what my Church says'. That's what is closing off those opportunities. But it makes life more difficult to have those opportunities.*

Stage 6: 'Selfless Faith'
[Universalizing Faith/The God-Grounded Self]

This book began with a quotation from the interview with 'Jane', the 79-year-old with undoubted Stage 6 characteristics. Here is another extract:

> *Interviewer: When you think of the future, how does it make you feel?*
> *Jane: The only thing that bothers me about the future, I think, is have I left everything as tidy as possible? Is the family all sort of settled alright? You have this feeling, and also the feeling that I think most couples think— who they hope will go first. And I mean as far as I am concerned I think it's much better if [my husband] goes first, because I think I could manage easier than he could. I've tried to get used to the idea over a period of years of what it would feel like to go into a home and I keep talking to myself about it. I've always felt that God has something for us to do as long as we are breathing, and so he would have something for people to do when they*

go into a home, but it's very few of them who can see it, and who can make something of the life inside. I always hope that I will be able to go on seeing that point. I had a friend who made a wonderful success—she went into a home at 88 and she died six months later, and the whole of that six months was spent looking after a blind and deaf lady, and Iris herself was 88! You know it was . . . I have always thought 'Don't let me ever forget that', because she was such a joy to be with, you know. . . .

Age: usually only in later life[11]; *a very rare stage.*
In this picture, we note, the little figure of the self has now disappeared, and the triangle and circles are drawn within a new boundary. Stage 6 is more of an extrapolation from Stage 5 than something discovered by research. Only 0.3% of Fowler's sample were scored as being at Stage 6. He draws examples of the type from recent hagiography—Mother Teresa of Calcutta, Dag Hammarskjöld, Martin Luther King. These are figures whose way of being in faith is essentially a relinquishing of the self, where the self is no longer the ultimate reference point. It has been 'abandoned' in favour of a grounding in ultimate Reality (for many religions, a grounding in God). Those who are at Stage 6 have found their selves by losing their selves. Fowler's description of the stage includes a vision of a sense of the unity of all things, through the multiplicity of faith and being. This is almost a mystical, spiritual unity; but its power is that of a uniting love for all. A Stage 6 person is in the world but not of the world. For him or her 'life is both loved and held to loosely' (*SF* 201).[12] Such figures may not survive long in this world. They give so much of themselves, and are vulnerable to the power of those whose values they challenge by their own valuing. It may be said that Stage 5 people see the world 'out there' as very much in need of 'redemption', but they also see the points of view of others too clearly to do anything about it. Stage 6 people, however, go out to transform that world. And they often die in the attempt.

These faith pilgrims are not perfect, morally or in any other sense. But they have a distinctively new faith and 'a new quality of freedom with the self and with others' (*FDPC* 76). The circle of their love, and their recognition of community, has widened to include the whole human race. Compared with Stage 5 this is what has been called a simplicity on the other side of complexity.[13] 'There is a union of opposites that is no longer experienced as paradoxical' (*LM* 89). This is revealed in the presence of what Fowler sometimes calls 'a relevant irrelevance'. There is something radically new here, something transcendent.

Stage 6 may be rare, but it represents a sort of logical progression of the widening of social perspective and 'decentration from self' that can be traced throughout the stages. The 'widening of vision and valuing' represented by each successive stage goes along with an increasing responsibility, awareness and depth of reflection.[14]

In another diagram, this one suggested by Northrop Frye, Fowler shows how this 'simultaneous process of *centring* and *de-centring*' occurs

in faith development. The 'increasingly *individuating* self' assumes the burden of understanding and maintaining its own vision of reality (distinct from that of others) and taking autonomous moral responsibility. At the same time 'at each stage a more inclusive account is taken of persons, groups, experiences and world views other than one's own' (*EIRE* 200). A person more and more becomes herself as she increasingly widens her circle of concern and truth-finding. To see the unity of everything 'out there', and to unite oneself with all people in their infinite variety, demands a 'person who has a non-egocentric unity' inside (*LM* 131). This is captured in the accompanying drawing.[15]

3

Is this Faith?

QUESTIONS AND CRITICISMS

In this chapter we shall attempt a more critical look at Fowler's account of faith development. Of course 'critical' does not here mean 'negative'. A critical person is one who judges or assesses ideas and practices. He or she will ask questions and reflect carefully on the answers, rather than 'jump to conclusions' either for or against an idea or argument. We include below some of the more frequently heard questions that are asked of faith development theory, with some attempt to respond to them.

Some of these questions pose difficulties for Fowler's account, and we should take note of them. It should also be said, however, that much of the neglect of faith development theory in this country is to be explained not so much by the strength of the arguments against it, as by the general neglect of developmental psychology coupled with the tendency of practical Christian educators to seek out only those things that promise a quick practical application.

Before we turn to a rehearsal of some basic questions that might be asked of faith development theory, we should record a cautionary comment directed to those for whom the temptation is to apply it enthusiastically and uncritically all over the place. Superficial assessment of people as being at one stage or another is easy, but dangerous. It is particularly dangerous for the cleric or teacher who sees himself as being one or two stages further 'advanced' than those committed to his charge. We should not judge too quickly what stage people are at. In-depth interviews can provide that sort of data. Passing conversations cannot.

But is this faith?

Fowler makes clear from the outset that he is studying a particular understanding of—or element in—faith. His emphasis on the form or structure of the processes of faith, rather than its content, is a central distinction. Structure, as we have seen, is an abstraction from the concrete reality of the life of faith, and sometimes it is rather difficult

36

to abstract it satisfactorily. Those who wish to limit the application of the word faith to a particular faith-content (e.g. 'religious faith') may of course still find Fowler's account of use in describing some part of, or element in, what *they* call faith. Many critics are worried by the use of the word 'faith' to cover non-religious positions and non-theistic views (i.e. viewpoints without a belief in God). On Fowler's view even 'idolatry is a form of faith'.[1] These critics may be willing to accept that faith is an attitude or orientation, but argue that it is an orientation towards *God* or some other 'religious object'. For some faith is only defined by its content: it is a response to and participation in God's revelation and salvation, or it is nothing.

Fowler's analysis of faith embraces other examples, however. Indeed he claims that it has universal range—wherever human beings are to be found, there is faith. As another writer has put it: faith is 'the prodigious hallmark of being human' and a 'fundamental human category'.[2] It isn't just restricted to religious people. On the contrary it is almost a defining characteristic of the human psyche. A number of critics find Fowler's account confusingly broad, covering virtually the whole of life and becoming indistinguishable from knowing in general.[3] But however much the theologian stresses a particular understanding of God, and therefore of faith in God, he must acknowledge a broader understanding of human orientation towards whatever is god (small 'g') for each individual. Everyone has their gods, but not all have faith in the one 'God and Father of Our Lord Jesus Christ'. The Bible itself talks of those whose 'god is the belly' (Philippians 3.19): those who value and rest their faith in their own appetites and desires (presumably they didn't worship a Great Stomach-in-the-Sky!). As Martin Luther put it, 'trust and faith of the heart alone make both God and idol' and 'whatever then thy heart clings to . . . and relies upon, that is properly thy god'. There are indeed 'many "gods" and many "lords" ' (1 Corinthians 8.5). Furthermore, it is clear that human 'knowing in general' is intimately involved in what may become for some a particular religious faith.

What is loss of faith?

Because faith is a human universal in Fowler's view, a *total* loss of *all* faith would be equivalent to ceasing to be truly a person. Can loss of faith be that total? Perhaps even the professed 'nihilist' believes in something. *Beginning* to slip down the slope towards the abyss of loss of human faith is enough, however, to provoke despair. We cannot live —or at least not really 'live'—without *some* centres of value and power and some orientation towards them, some focusing of our lives.[4]

Most Christians, however, understand something less radical when they say: 'He's lost his faith.' They mean that a person no longer rests his heart in God, Jesus or the Church: he no longer has 'faith in' these faith-contents. They may even mean rather less than this, namely that such a person no longer holds certain 'beliefs-that', that is certain 'beliefs about' God, Jesus or the Church. (This may still be compatible with having 'faith in' God, Jesus or the Church—it depends on the nature of the particular beliefs-about. Thus one can still trust in God the Creator, while denying that he created the universe in six days.) Fowler's account of conversion as a change in the content rather than the form of faith (see below) might involve a 'loss of faith' of this sort. But the periods of transition, during which we lose one form of faith before, or as, we take up another, are a better example of what Fowler would mean by loss of faith. These are temporary experiences although they can be traumatic enough: a limited taste of what total loss of faith might be. It should be noted that words like 'unfaithful' or 'faithless' are best reserved for theological comments on a particular person's faith-content (e.g. disobedience to or lack of trust in *God*).

What is conversion?

Conversion 'to'—or 'from' or 'within'—religion is an important phenomenon. It is often expressed as conversion into, or out of, a set of beliefs. But students of religion usually adopt a wider definition that better captures the sense of a radical turning or re-turning. Conversion is not just a change of beliefs, but a change in, or redirection of, the whole life. This involves a change in 'past ideas, attitudes, values or behaviour, more generally all four of these accompanied by intense feeling'.[5] This relates closely to a 'content-change', a change in the *what* of faith, which is recognized by Fowler as conversion. People are converted as they shift the focus of their lives to other centres of value, images of power and master stories (*SF* 281ff). This is a change in our 'gods', and for Fowler it can happen during any faith stage. St Ignatius of Loyola's conversion was a content-change of this nature. For at least some years after his conversion his 'soldierly' form of faith remained the same, but it was directed to a different goal and authority compared with its pre-conversion focus.

38

Some commentators argue, however, that in addition to this sort of change, conversion involves a change in structural stage, a redirection and reintegration of the human processes of trusting and valuing.[6] People are converted, they would say, to a new *way* of seeing things as well as to a new faith-content. Psychologists of religion, we may note, often focus on this form-change and treat conversion as a type of identity-formation in which a person comes to discover who she really is, who 'loves her' and where she 'fits in' in the world. Conversion thus unifies and integrates the self, particularly in the crucial periods of adolescence and middle age.[7] Fowler acknowledges that stage change may go along with content change, and that the one may precipitate the other, but he still prefers to 'reserve the term *conversion* for those sudden or gradual processes that lead to significant changes in the *contents* of faith' (*SF* 285). In Christian terms this is 'a recentring of our passion', by our 'making an attachment to the passion of Jesus the Christ'—'a loving, committed and ready-to-suffer passion for the in-breaking commonwealth of love' (*BABC* 140).

It is interesting that one commentator argues that Stage 2 to Stage 3 transition is a particularly important change, itself worthy of the name of conversion:

> The transition from law, death, and egocentrism to grace, life, and relationship—with others, and to a God who is gracious—fits the most familiar, traditional understanding of religious conversion.[8]

How deep is faith?

We often make distinctions between different people's faith using metaphors that are apparently drawn from the sea. Thus 'he has such a shallow faith', whereas 'her faith is so deep'.[9] Part of the implication of this language is that the *intensity* of a person's faith is important. While Fowler's scheme certainly recognizes that faith commitment may be slight or intense, any increase or decrease of intensity is not a part of faith stage change or conversion (faith-content-change), but something that cuts across both. The only exception to this seems to be in the more content-full Stage 6. Intensity is, however, an important additional element in any complete account of a person's faithing, and in what many people would understand by the phrase 'growth in faith', as is the rather different quality of *sincerity* (the extent to which a person's faith truly expresses that person in an honest fashion).

Do we go back as well as forward in faith development?

According to Fowler each stage represents a development from an earlier one—building on it and reworking its contents into the new form (this is sometimes described as a 'recapitulation' of the images, stories etc. of previous faith stages—cf. *SF* 288ff). But if I am now at Stage 4, might I return to the *form* of Stage 3? Might I 'regress' in faith? Sometimes Fowler suggests that this can happen, but it is usually assumed—and much of the evidence supports this view—that people 'move on' in faith, not backwards. Although psychoanalysts speak of regression, cognitive theorists tend to avoid the idea. If regression does occur it may be a temporary phenomenon, an attempt to adjust to a new stage by briefly using the style of an earlier one. Yet with advancing age changes in cognitive powers may force a reversion to earlier ways of being in faith. Only 'longitudinal research', however, in which the *same people* are charted over the years as they journey in faith, could answer the question one way or another. Such research takes very many years and little of it has been done. This is a weakness of faith development research to date, although some support can be drawn from longitudinal research into Kohlberg's moral stages.

Faith development: Is or ought?

Throughout his works Fowler insists that the faith development scheme is not an 'achievement scale' (*LM* 8). He argues that his stages of faith are intended essentially as *descriptions* of where people are, and not as *prescriptions* of where they ought to be. The stages do not indicate 'an increasing capacity for faithfulness or any other human virtue' (*M* 2). People can be mystically alive, Fowler claims, even at Stages 1 and 2. Saints might be at Stage 3, 4, 5 or 6. Each stage has its own integrity, value and completeness. Each stage can be regarded as fully Christian, in a moral, theological, spiritual or religious sense.[10]

It would be a pastoral and educational mistake, therefore, to seek to rush people through the stages. There is great danger in pushing people out of a stage without reference to the ways they currently actually think and relate. There are no shortcuts in faith development. It is only when people are 'trapped' in a faith stage that they have partly otherwise 'outgrown' (for example in their way of thinking), or when they have precociously 'advanced' beyond their actual psychological and social maturity, that the pastor or educator should step in to help them work on those aspects of their faithing that are out of step with the rest of their meaning-making (*SF* 114). Faith, says Fowler, is like a shawl (of meaning) that we knit and wrap around ourselves. It is not the job of the pastor or educator to slash at this with a knife or rip it from a person's shoulders. But sometimes the shawl starts to unravel of its own accord. And then we should step in to help: not by darning up the loose ends, but by rolling up the wool, standing by the wearer in his nakedness, and then encouraging him to knit a new shawl for himself.

On the other hand we should not insulate people from reality (as they begin to perceive it anew), or try to keep people at a faith stage which psychologically they are outgrowing, like the eleven-year-old atheist stuck at Stage 2 or the adolescent unable to cope with his new college world with his Stage 3 faith. There is always the danger that a person will 'over defend existing faith structures by screening out and "not-knowing" dissonant data' (*FSM* 67).[11] It is new experience that often leads to faith stage change, as and when the existing structures can no longer accommodate it. This causes a situation of conflict in which a person's faith is thrown off balance. Its form needs to change to restore some sort of equilibrium and with it a sense of 'coping'. Faith development is desirable under such circumstances.

Fowler often remarks wryly that, although only one third of one per cent of his sample 'arrived' at Stage 6, every group he speaks to shows most interest in this stage. This is perhaps not very surprising! The social sciences have offered us many developmental schemes that provide an overview of growing up. It is usual to present such schemes as essentially descriptive: straightforward, factual accounts of how people actually develop—of what actually *happens*. But they invariably contain a normative element as well, or at least we cannot stop ourselves treating them as normative—as accounts of what *should happen*. For where you can get to in development, we assume, is surely where you should end up. In the case of a train or car journey, for example, we usually think that it is better to have arrived than still to be on the way. Thus ideas of human development, like ideas of biological or social evolution, provide us with images of a future (even if it is for many an ideal and in practice unrealizable future) that operate rather like what philosophers used to call 'final causes', pulling us to themselves. It is the Good-Time-Coming or the Good-Thing-We-Are-Becoming, at least 'in hope', and to know it is to love it. It serves us as an image or symbol of what it is to have arrived, to have 'succeeded' in development. This is how we naturally think.

Presumably such an image of maturity or adulthood relates to what some psychologists have called a person's '*project*', which includes what I have uniquely to do and to become: my image of myself that has to be realized, actualized or 'individuated'. This is my possible future state. It is what I aspire to. And 'image' is the right word for it, for it has its home in the imagination. There it is fed not only by my sober observations of facts about my development and the nature of other adults, but also by stories and myths, fiction and fantasy—by films of Clint Eastwood as much as by books by Thomas Merton. Some aspects of this image are realizable—I *shall* become like this. Others are not. Some are recognized as having the status of an ideal. The *Manual for Faith Development Research* describes Stage 6 as 'a type of normative image of what human development can be' (*M* 178). Fowler elsewhere acknowledges that it was derived originally from a theological picture of 'radical monotheism' (belief in one God above and beyond the many penultimate 'gods' of value and power) and of the 'Kingdom of God' (*SF* 204ff). It is a *sort of* ideal, and fairly obviously it has a particular religious and theological colouring.

Fowler himself admits that each new stage is in some sense more adequate than the previous one, and there appears at first sight to be some tension here with the view that he is simply offering a description of how people actually develop. But how could it be otherwise? Valuation is built into all our language and our life, nothing is pure neutral description. As a matter of fact, Fowler seems to be saying, faith changes in these ways, and—provided that the movement comes at the appropriate time—a 'good job too'. We must recognize that we are not to press the stages into a GCSE-like grading scheme. Yet many people (but not all) will regard the later stages' form of social awareness, treatment of symbols and way of making a coherent picture of reality as 'better' than the ways of thinking, relating, understanding and meaning-making that are (inevitably) adopted in the different aspects of earlier stages. Their scope is wider; they are more able to cope with and adapt to new experiences; they take more into account. Human beings develop because they need to. 'The new way can account for things that the old ways no longer could.'[12] Thus, although 'each stage has a potential wholeness, grace, and integrity', yet also 'each stage represents genuine growth toward wider and more accurate response to God, and toward more consistently humane care for other human beings' (*FDF* 38f).

We *do* grow, and we *should* grow; for 'more developed structural stages of knowing are, in important ways, more comprehensive and adequate than the less developed ones' and 'make possible a knowing that in some senses is "more true"' (*SF* 101). But people at a later stage are still not to be regarded as having more intrinsic worth than those at an earlier one (*EIRE* 201, *CA* 196), as being more 'faithful' or more Christian. In one sense, then, Stage 1 or 2 is 'adequate' (= 'appropriate') for the young child's nature. But later stages can be said to be more adequate at meeting the demands and perceptions of the new experiences that come later. And these later stages have a broader base from which the diversity of the world may be better understood and encountered. So Fowler writes that 'of course there is a normativity' to developmental theories:

> Other things being equal, persons should be supported and encouraged to continue to engage the issues of their lives and vocations in such ways that development will be a likely result. (*FDPC* 80f)

Does it leave room for God?

One criticism often levelled at Fowler's work is that it gives a 'naturalistic' account, i.e. it leaves out God's role in changing a person's faith. Isn't faith essentially *God's* work? Isn't it a gift? It is certainly true that, like any other psychological analysis, Fowler's work focuses 'resolutely on the human side of the faith relationship'. But Fowler sees this human side as part of God's creative care for human beings, what he calls God's 'ordinary grace' that is built in to our human nature by God's original and ever-continuing act of giving. This, of course, is a particular theological viewpoint. But he also allows for other, more supernatural, gifts—God's additional activity by way of 'interventions of extraordinary grace'—which are not so expected or predictable. Because of this latter possibility, Fowler writes, 'it is difficult to speak simply or solely of faith as a developmental matter' (*SF* 303).

Commentators on Fowler are often willing to accept progression from Stage 1 through to Stage 5 as a natural process of development, but they do not regard movement to Stage 6 as being quite so natural. The negation of self-interestedness involved seems 'to require an explanation based on the initiatives of the Transcendent . . . the work of something like Grace' (*BABC* 74). This is usually proposed as a particular example of extraordinary, intervening, saving grace. It is sometimes further claimed that this sort of 'help' may in fact be needed throughout faith development so as to overcome human sin—our conscious or unconscious disposition to resist the workings of the natural, ordinary grace which is immanent in God's creation. But Fowler's own position, as expressed in his later work, is less 'interventionist' than these accounts of the matter. He writes of the working partnership (theologically '*synergy*') between human nature and the Spirit, and of grace as 'the presence and power of creative spirit working for human wholeness, . . . given and operative in creation from the beginning' (*ibid.*). On the whole this seems to be what he previously called 'ordinary grace', which comes from a sort of natural opening up to the Spirit. But he does continue to hint at something more 'extraordinary' in a breakthrough of Spirit in 'saving Grace' (note the capital letter!).

Is faith lonely?

Some would criticize Fowler's account as being too individualistic: concerned with *my* faithing, *my* way of making meaning and constructing a world to live in.[13] Christian educators in particular have often wanted to lay more emphasis on communal faith and the development of the Church, rather than on its individual members. The one-to-one research interview, and the individual life-story reflection it encourages, may sometimes seem a long way away from the concerns of those who work with small learning and activity groups or large worshipping assemblies.

But the individual *v.* communal dispute can only be resolved by declaring a truce. We are *both* individuals *and* members of (a wide range of overlapping) communities. In any case, faith development theory surely does take account of our communal life[14]—witness the discussion of the role of significant others, the horizontal dimension of trust and loyalty, the vertical dimension of *shared* commitments to faith-contents, and the degree to which people are said to be open to the 'community of being'. It is inevitable that, however faith is understood, it must be partly defined in terms of the individual.

Is faith development inevitable?

Many accounts of human development ('psychosocial' and 'life-cycle' perspectives) imply a necessary, inevitable sequence through which people move as they get older. Fowler, with other 'constructivists', has a different scheme. On his view people may and do—but equally may not and don't—reconstruct their ways of being in faith when they 'encounter disruptions' in their lives that their 'previous ways of making meaning cannot handle' (*BABC* 139). So Fowler writes, 'faith stage transitions are not automatic or inevitable. They may occur more slowly in one person or group than another, and some persons find equilibrium at earlier stages than do others' (*SF* 276). Thus we cannot predict with certainty at what faith stage a person will be, even if we know that person's chronological or mental age. And we cannot predict when, or if, they will move to another stage. 'Chronological age and maturation are necessary but not sufficient for stage transition' (*SFALC* 186).

In another sense, however, the pattern of faith stage *is* fixed and 'inevitable'. The railway lines of faith development are laid down, even if we cannot predict where the train has got to or how far it will go in its journey along them. Development, when it occurs, proceeds along the same sort of lines. Thus Fowler claims that each stage can only come after previous stages have been lived through, and we cannot 'miss out' a stage. 'Structural stages emerge in a predictable sequence, invariant in order' (*SFALC* 186). For some this is a controversial claim, which only a very full and careful research programme could justify. But it might be argued that Kohlberg's work has established some of Fowler's aspects as constituting an invariant sequence. Furthermore there is in some cases a logical requirement of sequence in that some aspects of some stages can only take the form they do if other developments have happened (for example world coherence and symbolic understanding is dependent on the development of a certain form of reasoning).

Theology or science?

This is perhaps an unfair and unkind way of putting the question! It fits with the supposition that theology is armchair speculation brashly arrived at before examining the evidence and then imposed on whatever facts dare to turn up, whereas science cautiously labours to verify tentative hypotheses and is always ready to be proved wrong. That picture is true neither of all science nor of at least some theology. But for the moment let us allow the question to stand in this stark form.

The difficulty is that both theology and science (psychology) have something to say about the nature of faith. 'Fowler wears two hats and speaks to two audiences.'[15] His account clearly is heavily indebted to theological accounts (especially that of H. Richard Niebuhr) of what faith is and should be, and of the variety of types of faith. He was also influenced by psychological theories about development in human thinking, moral judgement and perspective taking. These theories had their own relationship to experiment and observation ('empirical study'), but by the time Fowler took them up they had already developed a life of their own—as theories tend to do. Armed with these theological reflections and empirically-related theories, Fowler and his associates then looked at the facts of faith. Is it worrying or surprising, that the facts turned out to fit the interpretations (while, of course, modifying and extending them)? Fowler's theory is so broad and complex that it might be asked whether fairly general interviews could produce the sort of evidence that could directly validate or invalidate it. It is a theory which certainly contains many assumptions, including assumptions about the 'structure' of faith, its aspects, and what constitutes a faith stage.

Every theory contains assumptions. Some of them are bound to be untestable, for not everything can be tested—and certainly not all at the same time. But their existence in this case should lead us to be cautious in presenting Fowler's scheme as 'proven'. In the present book we have opted for a less ambitious claim. We hope to show that faith development theory is interesting and (often) illuminating. Whatever the strength of the main planks—and the small nails—of its edifice, at the very least it helps us to recognize that the form of a person's faith does *change.* And it leads us to expect that this change is to a degree predictable, which gives the theory considerable practical value.

A related criticism is whether Fowler has not produced a rather Western, liberal, middle-class, 'highbrow' or intellectual account of faith, an accusation that is often also applied to Kohlberg's view of morality. Despite claims that the faith stages can be found in a variety of cultures,[16] we cannot ignore the point that Western, liberal, middle-class, intellectuals (usually male[17]) are on the whole doing the finding! Certainly Fowler speaks of his account as fitting those who have had a Western-style education. But squeaky-clean, theoretical 'neutrality' is impossible in these areas. Fowler's perspective on faith is bound to be *his* perspective, his way of seeing things. Instead of worrying about how 'objective' it is, we should perhaps try looking at people through his spectacles and see what *we* see. Or is that being too uncritical?

Is Fowler's research good enough?

Fowler's research is based on several hundred interviews lasting up to three hours each in which children (from 3½ years), adolescents and adults (up to age 84) are encouraged to answer such questions as the following: 'What relationships seem most important for your life?', 'What is the purpose of human life?', 'Are there symbols or images or rituals that are important to you?' (*SF* 311, the questions were modified for children). 'Though respondents often voluntarily answer in specifically religious terms, religion as an issue and context is not explicitly introduced until the last quarter of the interview' (*FSM* 66). The responses are recorded, transcribed, coded and scored according to criteria relating to the different aspects (see our Chapter 1) and stages (Chapter 2) of faith. Thus, for example, 'Stage 2 is able to make the distinction between fantasy and reality, and between the symbol and the thing symbolized' (*M* 101), and 'A concern with general rules, laws and norms is explicit at Stage 4' (*M* 149). The questions, the criteria for scoring and the accounts of what constitute any particular stage are all open to criticism, but this is a rather technical matter.

Social scientists may be particularly sceptical about some of the accounts given of the early and late stages of faith development, because of the difficulties of assessing young children, and the fairly limited information produced about Stages 5 and 6. Additionally it has been claimed that the expectation that 'transitional' people (those between stages) should show more anxiety or alienation is not always fulfilled. This may be a problem with the way people are recognized as transitional, however, or it may be answered by the counter-claim that transition can often also be exhilarating. The way that the scoring of answers is 'averaged out' to give a stage level, the difficulty of assessing form of faith from people's content-filled conversations, and the large number of respondents that are designated as being 'transitional' are points to be borne in mind when assessing the value of the research. More significantly, developmental claims cry out for the support of 'longitudinal research' (interviewing the same people over a number of years), and this work has not yet been done by students of faith development.

In a careful study of Fowler's research methods, Nelson and Aleshire[18] broadly endorsed his methodology, despite some unease in a number of areas.[19] The authors were positive about large parts of the research methodology and argued that:

(a) Fowler, quite properly, treats his data very tentatively;

(b) the research is adequate 'for the proposal of a theory' (p190), if not for its confirmation (although 'to some extent this theory can be disconfirmed', p200)[20]; and

(c) 'his research methods are, by and large, quite consistent with his structuralist approach' (p199).

While commenting wryly that 'at each point of his research Fowler has opted for the difficult', they note that 'the best evaluation of empirical research . . . is more empirical research' (p199). Armchair criticism can be as useless as armchair theorizing. Fowler has at least done some work! The authors cited concluded with this question:

Does the developmental journey Fowler traces 'ring true' with people who take seriously their constructions of meaning, values, relationships and centres of power? (p200)

The present writers would agree that there is a great deal that is of value in Fowler's research findings and the theory based thereon. We believe that the developmental journey he traces will 'ring true' for many others.

Is it all too rational?

Many critics feel that Fowler's account of faith is rather unbalanced in that it lays too much stress on the cognitive (thinking, knowing) dimension of faith, and too little on the dimension of affect (feeling, emotion). One early critic asserted bluntly: 'To him faith is a philosophy of life.'[21] As Fowler interweaves the different contributions of other researchers, and opens up the varied 'windows into faith' that are constituted by the faith aspects, it might seem that it is the processes of thinking and moralizing and the influences of Piaget and Kohlberg, rather than more psychoanalytic insights, that dominate his work. A reader could be excused for arguing: 'Despite all he says about faith as relationship, at the end of the day how we think and reason appear to be the most significant element in faith.' After all, it is these factors that hold us back or release us to go forward in the development of a number of the other aspects of faith. Yet it should be noted once again that there is no simple and automatic correlation between mental age and faith stage. Mental age may be a necessary factor for some stage changes, but it is not a sufficient one (i.e. it is not enough on its own).

Nevertheless there is some truth in the criticism. Intellectual ability ('intelligence') seems to have a considerable influence in Fowler's scheme on the way we hold our faith. His account often gives us too intellectualist an account of faith, not least when he speaks of Stage 4 faith as involving a 'critical choosing of one's beliefs, values and commitments' (*BABC* 62). Is it all too rational?

Fowler's account fits more closely an interpretation of faith as 'faith-knowing' (his phrase), as our way of making meaning and understanding reality, than it does faith as a felt attitude to life or a deep orientation of our hopes, fears and desires. But the cognitive dimension *is* important, and it does seem to be the case that as people come to think differently and to become conscious and self-critical of their beliefs and values, so the whole of their being-in-faith changes. Intelligence *is* a factor in this. We are thinking beings, as well as feeling ones. Our feeling certainly affects our thinking but Fowler's account reminds us that thinking has its own, peculiarly pervasive, effect in the life of faith. Faith is not—and we should not pretend that it is— the same as *knowledge* (as product or result). But *knowing* (as process or activity) is still an important component of faith. Faith is not *only* a philosophy of life, but then Fowler doesn't say that it is. And religious faith certainly has that dimension, among others.

Faith itself is to some extent—and for many in large part—a matter of how we think about and understand Reality. It is how we make meaning in our lives. Now 'meaning making' is often presented as a merely cognitive matter. But Fowler, Kegan[22] and others see it as involving the whole person. Kohlberg himself denies that moral judgements are merely cognitive—they 'often involve strong emotional components'.[23] Fowler's own work acknowledges the limitation of the 'relatively narrow understanding of cognition' (*SF* 102) provided by Piaget and others. This underlies his attempt to broaden this 'logic of rational certainty' into a less objective and disinterested 'logic of conviction' (cf. note 12 to Chapter 1). He thus advocates a 'broader form of reason . . . those fundamental constructs of the human imagination which give meaning to life' (*CA* 177). Whether he has been wholly successful in this is of course open to question.[24]

The 'structuralist' approach of people like Fowler posits frameworks or patterns in the mind ('structures') that we bring to our experience and understanding of reality—actively forming, organizing or 'structuring' that experiential knowledge. Cognitive developmentalists claim to have shown how these structures develop over time through a fixed sequence of development in reasoning, moralizing—and faithing. These claims about the existence and development of such structures or schemata are open to theoretical and experimental criticism, and recent accounts by developmentalists are less dogmatic and more tentative than popular surveys (like the present book) can show. We do not wish to be dogmatic about faith development theory, and neither does Fowler. It *is* possible to view the work of Fowler and others as a useful tool with which to poke into the mechanics of faith, or (to change the metaphor) as a torch bringing illumination into certain dark corners of the religious life. Readers may do this without committing themselves to all the theoretical implications of these theories, or to the full details of the research 'findings'. While more careful empirical work is always needed, and theoretical criticism is absolutely essential, some of the central themes of faith development are too important—and many of them too well supported by experience—to be cavalierly ignored.

What about religious experience?

This is a question that is closely related to the previous one. 'Religious experience' is a term of wide-ranging meaning. It can be applied to those affective states of joy, acceptance, penitence, assurance, awe, thankfulness and concern that are an integral part of the religious life. This may be described as 'subjective' religious experience. These attitudes/emotions/feelings may be part and parcel of any faith stage, and directed towards any faith-content. It may be that Fowler's account pays less attention to them than they deserve, but he gives them more of a place than some traditional devotional manuals which encourage us to discount them entirely as unreliable and ephemeral.

But the more frequently heard criticism is that the faith development scheme says too little about religious experience in another sense—religious experience as an experience of God, the Spirit or the risen Christ, or as a less determinate 'sense of presence' or experience of unity with the divine. This is sometimes called 'objective' religious experience. Some research claims to show that even fairly young children have such experiences, indeed that these experiences may be more common among the young.[25]

Fowler's stage theory can accommodate such claims about our religious experience of God. Of course people will be open at various stages to all sorts of different means by which they come to know

God (religious experience, revelation, the learning of Scripture and tradition, arguments for God's reality). Two points may be made here. Firstly we should recognize that there often is change in the ways that people understand and relate to these things and to God, for example by changes in their reasoning and their understanding of symbols. We should further note the changes in how they recognize others as authorities for their own faithing. Objective religious experience can, and does, come at any stage. But it will be received, interpreted and *used* in different ways at different stages. And, as with more 'secular' experiences, *what* we come to believe and be aware of will then help to change the *form* of our future believing and awareness. Such radical changes in the contents of one's faith can lead to structural stage change.

ALTERNATIVES TO FOWLER?

Others have hypothesized some sort of 'faith development' scheme. To conclude this chapter we will consider three other viewpoints (all American and contemporary). Readers may find them illuminating not least in their similarities to, and differences from, Fowler's account. But they should note that all of them represent rather 'armchair speculation' as their authors have not engaged in any careful, systematic, empirical research to test them.[26]

John Westerhoff

One of the best known of these schemes is that offered by John H. Westerhoff III, the popular writer on Christian education. He speaks of 'four distinctive styles of faith', acknowledging his indebtedness to Fowler's work.[27] At one point Westerhoff writes of the styles of faith as being like the annual rings of a tree. A tree with one ring is 'a complete and whole tree' and a tree with three rings 'is not a better tree but only an expanded tree' (*WOCHF* 90). Like a tree we expand from one style of faith to another slowly and gradually, always bearing within ourselves our earlier styles of faith.

Fowler also recognizes that adults are still six years old 'inside', but his emphasis lies more with the *results* of that faithing and the *contents* of the earlier faith stage. These are the things that tend to be carried over and that need to be reworked as we adopt a new faith form. Each Fowler stage marks the rise of new capacities and strengths that are added to and 'recontextualize' earlier patterns without 'negating or supplanting them' (*SF* 274). Westerhoff's position sounds similar:

51

As we expand in faith we do not leave one style of faith behind to acquire a new style but, on the contrary, each new style is added to the previous ones. (*WOCHF* 90f)

But Westerhoff draws slightly different implications from his view. For him the re-adoption of earlier styles of faith is a simple matter. It can occur at any time if the needs of an earlier style of faith (e.g. for experiences of trust or of belonging) cease to be met. Progression only occurs when these needs *are* satisfied; and the subject then moves on to satisfy other, developing concerns.

Westerhoff's tree-trunk analogy may be pictured thus:

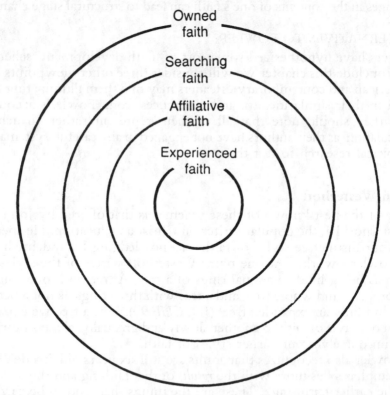

The four Styles of Faith that Westerhoff postulates are as follows. They can be fairly readily correlated with Fowler's stages.

1. *Experienced Faith* is the active and responding faith of the pre-school years and early childhood, which is experienced in the child's

relationships to others. (Presumably this would be equivalent to Fowler's Stages 0 and 1.)

2. *Affiliative Faith* is the 'belonging faith' of later childhood/early adolescence, dominated by the religious affections, significant others and their stories, and the authority of a community. (This may cover Fowler's Stages 2 and 3.)

3. *Searching Faith* is common in late adolescence/early adulthood and comprises (i) doubt and/or critical judgment (as the 'religion of the head' becomes equal in importance to the 'religion of the heart'), (ii) experimentation with alternative understandings and ways, and (iii) the need for commitment to persons and causes—the last two elements sometimes giving the impression of fickleness as various ideologies are experimented with in rapid succession. (Is this the transition between 3 and 4?)

4. *Owned Faith* integrates the previous stages into a witnessing faith stance, a new personal faith-identity that is expressed in both word and deed. (This is equivalent to Fowler's Stage 4.)

Unlike Fowler, Westerhoff describes faith development movement itself as 'conversion' (cf. *WOCHF* 98).

In a more recent book,[28] Westerhoff admits that he now prefers to speak of *three 'pathways'* or 'trails' to God, which may be travelled 'at any time, in any order', adding that we may 'return to any trail at will'.[29] Here he combines the first two styles of faith into a description of the 'slow, easy path' of the nurturing *Affiliative-Experiencing Way,* which he contrasts with the more demanding, rocky road of the *Illuminative-Reflective Way* where 'there is no marked trail' for the increasingly independent questers (this is clearly the time for 'searching faith'). The third path, which combines the first two, is the *Unitive-Integrating Way*:

> On this complex path the community encourages persons to move back and forth between the two previous ways and thereby create a new way. (p45)

Interdependent persons on this path combine intellectual and intuitive ways of knowing, become aware of pluralism, and are 'open to other possibilities' and the value of the other paths. This account thus sounds like a development of Westerhoff's 'owned faith' into something very reminiscent of Fowler's Stage 5.

The strength of Westerhoff's view probably lies in the vividness of his metaphors (e.g. of the tree-trunk), and the way in which he relates faith development to the processes of Christian learning and discipleship. Westerhoff's contribution may be viewed to a large extent as a popular reinterpretation of Fowler's research.

Gabriel Moran

This religious educationalist's 'theory of religious education development' recognizes three stages:

1. *Simply religious.* Young children may simply 'be religious', and religious education at this stage has more to do with providing warmth, stability and aesthetic form than offering instruction in belief. 'At this time, whatever is education is religious education',[30] for 'religious' here—a very broad term—stresses particular qualities and characteristics of a child's physical and 'visual/mythical' education.

2. *Christian (or Jewish or Muslim)* is an intermediary stage in which we get (through catechetics or Christian education) the 'solid substance' of a particular religious tradition, its historical narratives and traditional practices, and the intellectual systematizing of its theology.

3. *Religiously Christian (Jewish, Muslim)* is the adult stage in which the childhood religious position is placed in a new, globally-ecumenical, 'richer context of understanding'; when the religious element of early childhood 're-emerges in adulthood . . . now itself qualified and specified by Christian, Jewish, or Muslim elements' (p191). To move from Stage 2 to Stage 3 involves some relativizing of the knowledge gains of Stage 2, through journeying/inquiry followed by a shifting and refocusing—a 'centring'—of a person's religious life.

Again this is a speculative and very generalized account. It may be useful in its emphasis on the appropriately different understandings we should have of religious education at different stages, and as a reflective gloss on Fowler's more technical account—particularly of the transition to what we have here called 'balanced faith' (Fowler's Stage 5).

Sam Keen

The theologian Sam Keen was the co-author (with Fowler) of *Life Maps* (*LM* 103ff). There he criticizes Fowler for advocating a 'professorial typology of human development' which is too masculine and intellectual, 'in which everybody ends up like a professor with a coherent view of the world'. By contrast, Keen emphasizes the wish-desire-fantasy, feeling and sensual elements of faith as *trust* ('which is a gut word, not a head word'). He rejects the attempt to build (a certain interpretation of) a moral dimension into the notion of trust, which he defines as a 'yielding of the illusion of control and a concomitant loss of character and transformation of personality'. Trust is inconsistent; it tolerates plurality; it is passionate and compassionate; it integrates opposites (like masculine and feminine). But it is not itself a controlling, unifying thing. Keen claims to discern five stages or 'dimensions' of life, each of which remains in a person who has advanced beyond it. They are:

1. *The Child*—a period of dependence and affiliation, of accepting the given culture (equivalent to Fowler's Stage 1).
2. *The Rebel*—is counterdependent, defining herself against parents and culture.
3. *The Adult*—can say 'Yes' (with the Child) and 'No' (with the Rebel). She has established her character, built up a 'character armour' and affirms the values of the culture. Few go beyond this stage of ego strength, moving 'beyond the crust of culture' to:
4. *The Outlaw*—who kills the old authorities and seeks autonomy, questioning the old values—for 'love is prior to the law'. This is a dangerous stage and can lead to amorality or worse if the simple pleasures of life are also rejected. In meditating on death progress can lead on to:
5. *The Lover or the Fool* (equivalent to Fowler's Stage 6). This is an incommunicable stage of enlightenment: 'the world has ceased to be a problem to be solved and has become a mystery to be enjoyed'. No longer concerned with the question 'Who am I', in this 'life beyond character' the lover/fool trusts and loves. In a passage so arresting as to be worth quoting at length, Keen writes:

> The clue to the personality of the lover is that vulnerability and compassion have replaced defensiveness and paranoia. The lover has come back to the basic trust of the child. S/he is primarily *with*. The vision of second innocence turns the world from a battleground into an arena where divine forces are playing out a love drama. The seeming plurality of things only masks a deeper unity. The communion of all beings is the hidden truth. The lover can say 'all is one' and know what s/he is talking about.

It is only after the tragedy of disease, evil, and death has been wrestled with that authentic love begins to emerge. I suspect the 'wisdom' of twenty-year-old children who have had no encounter with the raw side of life. When they say 'All is one', they don't know what they are talking about. . . . You cannot lose an ego that you have not constructed. Character armour must be built before it can be destroyed. . . . The whole notion of teaching young people to be saints before they have been sinners is ridiculous. The yogis and spiritual masters who advocate wall-to-wall spiritual disciplines for adolescents have no respect for the wisdom of time. They try to teach wisdom before folly has been tasted. They train children to give Sunday school affirmations of love before they have discovered the depths of their untrust. (*LM* 123)

Fowler's careful response to Keen's thoughts are worth reading (*LM* ch 4). Keen's own lasting contribution probably lies in his vivid sense of the role of the passions in faith and of the significance of 'the wisdom of time'. These emphases should have a considerable part to play in any account of the development of faith. Despite his apparent differences, Keen's insights can to a large extent be accommodated by Fowler's theory provided that that theory does not place undue emphasis on the intellectual and controlling elements of faith.

In what sense are these accounts 'alternatives to Fowler'? On one view they cannot be described as such at all, for they are not properly structured theories offered with supporting evidence. Nor do they provide us with much detail. Some of them are not really 'stage theories' at all, perhaps deliberately so. But like Fowler's work, they may prove illuminating when set against the reader's own experience of her own and others' faith development. Because of their narrower breadth of theoretical content and range of practical application, however, they offer no serious rivalry to Fowler's own account.[31]

4

How is Faith?

INTRODUCTION

We now turn our attention to some of the practical implications of faith development thinking. These practical concerns relate to three rather different areas: context, activities, and the people themselves.

Faith development has practical implications for various *contexts* in which people live their lives, and live out their Christian lives. The context might be that of the home and family, the day school or other educational institution (including theological college), the various contexts of formal Christian education (Sunday school, confirmation classes, adult discussion groups, all-age learning experiences etc.), or other Church and life contexts (Church councils and synods, the work place etc.).

Among the *activities* for which faith development theory has implications we may include a large number of individual and group behaviours which carry a Christian label. Examples would include pastoral care, evangelism, teaching, spiritual counselling and formation, 'media religion' and worship. Particular styles of Christian tradition and being may also be included under this broad heading—for the handing on of a tradition is itself an activity, and our particular ways of being Christian are revealed and expressed in our Christian behaviour. Thus we might pay attention to faith development and liberalism, faith development and the conservative Christian, or faith development and the fundamentalist. Catholic and evangelical emphases may also be of significance here.

The third area of concern is that of the *people* undergoing faith development: young or older children; early or late adolescents; young, middle-aged or older adults; people stabilized at different stages and people in transition between stages.

These different logical areas—context, activities and people—can be used as a grid on which we may position a particular practical topic. Any given concrete topic will relate to more than one of the areas. Thus 'confirmation' usually relates to the *context* of confirmation training and the *activities* of teaching and worship, and (in the Church

57

of England at least) it happens to *people* who are mainly young adolescents. Our three logical areas are best represented, therefore, like three dimensions of a cube—height, depth and breadth. Any position in the cube (any topic) can be specified by plotting it on each of these dimensions:

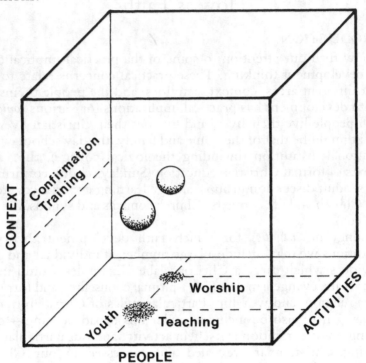

In what follows we shall not explicitly refer to this context/activities/people matrix, but we suggest that it might be a useful classificatory scheme to bear in mind when discussing particular concrete topics. The topics we have chosen by no means exhaust the range of possibilities, but we hope that they will show something of the practical implications of faith development theory.

CONFIRMATION

Fowler asks us to 'rethink confirmation in the light of faith development theory', as well as thinking about the Church's marking of other critical times in our life (*FDPC* 117). Certainly reflection on faith development should make us think more carefully about what is involved in an 'adult commitment' to Christianity, whether this be marked only by a once-for-ever confirmation, baptism or Church membership ritual, or also by a repeated ritual (as in the Methodist Annual Renewal of Covenant service). It should also give us pause before endorsing the common Anglican practice of offering confirmation to everyone at the age of twelve. Other denominations may find that their own practices of confirmation, or indeed of believer's baptism, may benefit from further reflection informed by the faith development framework. Christian education for Church membership needs to latch on to the implications of this work.

It is easy enough to spot the 'problem of confirmation', but more difficult to know what to do about it. Faith development theory might suggest that if confirmation is viewed as a time of personal commitment then it is most appropriate at Stage 4. Alternatively it may be viewed as a ritual marking the transition from Stage 3 to Stage 4: from the 'heteronomous faith' of those who have their faith defined by others, to the 'autonomous' faith of those who make (or who feel they are making) responsible faith choices for themselves and act upon them. Confirmation may then perhaps be appropriately viewed as a move from being (only) a disciple to being (also) an apostle.

The difficulty with these proposals, however, is that not everyone by any means makes the transition from Stage 3 to Stage 4, and certainly not in early adolescence. There are, it would seem, two alternatives. *Either* (i) confirmation should be delayed or withheld until a certain faith stage is reached, as Fowler himself seems to suggest: 'the act of joining the Church—even for those socialized from childhood into Christian faith in the Church—needs to be a post-adolescent event' (*PF* 17); *or* (ii) confirmation should be interpreted in different ways for different people at a variety of ages and stages. It is this latter practice that is usually followed: witness the difference between the Church's treatment of child/adolescent and adult confirmation candidates. Thus when we confirm at the age of 12 or 13 the act might be seen as a rite which 'authenticates transition from Stage 2 to Stage 3'.[1] For adults, however, it has a very different significance.

FAITH DEVELOPMENT AND SPIRITUALITY

'Spirituality' has become something of a growth industry in recent decades, both in the Churches and in schools. In formal education the importance of the spiritual growth of the child has been recently underscored by the 1988 Education Reform Act's recognition of this sort of development as one of the aims of school education in England and Wales, along with the child's moral, cultural, mental and physical development. The precise meaning of 'spiritual' in this context is not, however, defined.

According to one definition, spirituality comprises:

> those attitudes, beliefs, practices which animate people's lives and help them to reach out towards super-sensible realities.[2]

It might be understood, then, to include all sorts of attitudes and values (trust, concern, compassion, awe and wonder, tolerance, sense of duty etc.), which may or may not take an explicitly religious form. In the Church, of course, attention will be focused on the religious content and orientation of these attitudes and values. In both Church and school faith development theory may be seen as relating to the development of such a spirituality, at least as far as its *form* is concerned. This will be closely related to affective education that fosters the emotional life (its expression, depth and control), and those skills and capacities which relate to the exercise of human imagination, empathy and reflectiveness.[3]

SPONSORING FAITH

Fowler argues that there are no shortcuts to Christian commitment and growth in faith. It is the Christian's job to stand—or, better, walk—alongside others where they are, on their particular faith journeys. We can, however, offer ourselves as sponsors for the faith of others: walking part of the way with them, sharing the same view of the road and the same map and compass. Spiritual direction and spiritual nurture involve a forming of mind and heart that can best be seen as taking place on the road of faith. This draws on the image of Jesus teaching his disciples by word, acted parable and deed as they follow along behind him on the road to Jerusalem. The road of Christian formation is a life-journey of the development of a *form* of faith, as well as a pilgrimage that often leads the searcher through different ideas and images of the divine (i.e. of faith-*content*). Sponsorship is as important for this walk as it is for any fund-raising charitable marathon. 'Churches', Fowler writes, 'need to expect and provide support for ongoing adult development in faith' (*FSM* 79).

Some churches have adopted practical strategies to help those who have been confirmed to tread the way of faith with a mentor or fellow pilgrim. This can be of enormous value in a young person's own faith development journey. One such method, called 'Bus Stop', has been adopted by the Anglican Diocese of Salisbury. Hugh Disley writes:

> Bus Stop is a new approach aimed at young people who have already been through confirmation. The concept is that of undergoing a set of challenges which they have set for themselves under various headings. These challenges are interpreted and set in a Christian context and recorded and reflected upon.

> In order to get young people to be able to reflect upon their challenges in a Christian context they choose a member of the congregation who works on a one-to-one basis with them throughout the year of challenges, and helps to set their challenges and reflect upon the outcomes.

THE CONGREGATION

Recently there has been a lot of interest in the role of the worshipping congregation in Christian nurture,[4] and its spiritual and theological ethos.[5] Fowler introduces two related concepts that are of significance here: the congregation's modal development level and its climate of developmental expectation.

(a) *The modal developmental level* of the congregation is the 'average expectable level' of faith development of the adult members of a congregation. It is 'the conscious or unconscious image of adult faith toward which the educational practices, religious celebrations and patterns of governance in a community all aim' (*SF* 294). It operates as a 'kind of magnet', and Christian nurture is targeted to it—but not beyond it. (Fowler comments that for most middle-class churches in America it can best be described as Stage 3 faithing.[6]) This is related to Fowler's second notion.

(b) *A climate of developmental expectation* within a congregation is most important. By this Fowler does not mean that a congregation should be 'a hothouse garden, seeking to rush persons from one stage of faith to the next' (*SF* 296), but rather that it should provide nurturing help, rites of passage and opportunities for service 'that call forth the gifts and emergent strengths of each stage of faith'. The issue here is how far a congregation *expects* people to change, and in particular to change in the form of their faith, as they grow older and undergo different experiences.

For Fowler, at least, the appropriate 'stage level of aspiration for a public church' is Stage 5 faith (*FDPC* 97), for it is this stage which can best keep a congregation open-ended toward continuing growth. It is only in the stages beyond Stage 3, Fowler claims, that the intention of Christian faith for adult individual commitment is properly captured (*PF* 17, cf. *FDEC* 144). Here again we find normative emphases in faith development theory. For Fowler, we recall, 'other things being equal, persons should be supported and encouraged' to work at the issues of their lives and vocations 'in such ways that development will be a likely result' (*FDPC* 80f).

But the *variety* of faith stages to be found in a congregation must not be overlooked, or underplayed. Instead of worrying about future faith development, we should perhaps recognize and rejoice in this present variety. All God's people, after all, are saints—at least in the New Testament sense. And a truly universal (catholic) Church should include them all. The only cloud on such a horizon would be that those individuals who are at, or are capable of, Stage 5 may well experience difficulties if they find themselves members of a predominantly Stage 3 congregation.[7]

FAITH AND THE FAMILY

Some of Fowler's 'aspects of faith' (perspective-taking, locus of authority, and the perception of the limit of one's faith community) are clearly important aspects of our interpersonal relationships within the community of the family as well as of the Church. In addition to these, we may note other areas of overlap between faith development and family life.

In particular we should recognize that the family has its own developmental history, which is affected by—but not reducible to—the faith development of its individual members.[8] Faith development theory has at least this much in its favour: it makes us more aware of, and responsive to, *all* kinds of change—including the development of our families.

Further, a family is an inter-generational unit which comprises people at different stages, with different ways of being–in–faith. What are the problems and possibilities of Christian nurture in such a context? How can we be fair to our children and their stages of development, while being sufficiently open-ended to their likely future movement in faith? Can we recognize that we too are changing, perhaps from Stage 4 to

Stage 5 just as our children move from Stage 3 to Stage 4! Grandparents, we have noted, who can be expected to have changed most, are often better at coping with the changes of children and adolescents than are their parents. Perhaps this is what Fowler means by his claim:

> If their adolescent or near-adult children cannot, for the present, use Stage 5's new found playfulness in faith, his/her grandchildren— or other children, youth or younger adults in the community of faith—will soon take it seriously as liberating and welcome sponsorship. (*PF* 16f)

The family is often used as a metaphor for the Church: compare Jesus's words in Mark 3.34f and much familiar ecclesiastical rhetoric. This sort of language raises important questions about the notion of community in both family and Church. Herbert Anderson's description of family life as 'being separate together'[9] may be important here. In both family and Church we need one another *and* we need to be ourselves. Part of 'being ourselves' is being allowed to see, feel, think and relate at our appropriate faith stage. Where there is pressure to conform or be subordinate, development may be hindered. This pathological situation may last even as long as parents are alive—hence instances of development in older people when elderly parents die, or more generally when older members of a family die and young adults in the family blossom. If the atmosphere in a 'parish family' is authoritarian, development may be similarly thwarted. From the above comments it is clear that 'family' could usefully serve as a term for church members to explore, so as to uncover their different understandings of symbol.

Being a member of the family means that my way of being in faith needs to relate to, and interact with, the ways of faith of all the others. John Westerhoff writes:

> Without interaction between and among the generations, each making its own unique contribution, Christian community is difficult to maintain.[10]

Those at earlier faith stages tend to see members of the family in terms of their own relations with them, which usually means what the others do for them or how they are treated by them. It is only as they move on to another stage that they see others in the family as people in their own right, and themselves as having the responsible task of taking account of others.

Fowler himself illustrates his triadic model of faith—as involving (1) myself relating to (2) other people and (3) our shared centres of value and power—with the pattern that obtains in a family (*SF* 17). In the deepest of senses, families are crucially important for the formation of faith. The family has its own 'story' or formative myths that help to bind it together as a community—what might be called a 'narrative community'. We may note how birthdays, anniversaries and other family celebrations and rituals all draw on and reinforce this sense of a shared faith-content, despite the very different ages and stages of faith-form of the different members of the family. These shared rituals 'are sacramental. . . . They convey a sense of love, grace, worth, and meaning to life' (*N* 4). It is in the family that our faith is first formed, and for most people it is in the context of a family that it continues to develop.

'MEDIA RELIGION'

Fowler inveighs against television evangelists and others in his own country who 'have mastered the art of addressing the secularizing religious hungers of Synthetic-Conventional [Stage 3] folk' (*SF* 164). 'Tele-evangelists' offer a new set of external authorities while combining an appeal to the old Christian symbols with a theology of 'vicarious interpersonal warmth and meaning'. This 'parody of authentic Christianity' tries to keep people at Stage 3, lest they think for themselves and do their own religious shopping. Such a strategy has obvious benefits for the profit margins of the organizations involved in selling such media religion. 'Authentic Christianity', presumably, would be less able to maintain such product allegiance, as it would be open to the possibility of people moving on and giving up this particular kind of religious belonging.

With the de-regulation of broadcasting in Britain, it may be that television religion on lines somewhat similar to the American model will increasingly be experienced here. In which case its implications for the religious development of individuals should be borne in mind by those who share Fowler's analysis of the situation. Stage 3 media religion may create particular problems for those viewers who are at Stage 5.

FUNDAMENTALISM

The complex social and religious movement known as 'fundamentalism' possesses a variety of different dimensions. Theologically fundamentalists believe that the Bible is 'inerrant'—that is it contains no errors at all (not even of a minor historical or scientific kind). The position has, therefore, an all-or-nothing structure. Should a single error be discerned in Scripture, logic demands that the fundamentalist principle be treated as conclusively falsified. Hence the concern of fundamentalists to protect the Bible against *all* critical scholarship.

But there is much more to fundamentalism than this. Fundamentalism is wedded to a particular set of 'conservative' interpretations of the Bible and of basic Christian doctrines and fundamental theology. It rejects so-called 'liberal' reinterpretations or critiques of the theology of God's activity, particularly in history (the 'problem of miracle' etc.), as well as many contemporary moral, social and political views and practices.[11] Protestant fundamentalism often appears as a Scripture-only position, recoiling from the 'human traditions' of theology, Church councils or liturgy. But fundamentalism itself is a sort of tradition. What it 'passes on' (which is all that 'tradition' means) is a particular way of understanding the Bible, a particular set of fundamental doctrinal and ethical beliefs, and (often) particular ways of praying, worshipping, finding Christian authority, and so on. It might be said that some fundamentalist Churches have as part of their tradition 'a tradition of dispensing with tradition' (that is, of course, dispensing with *other people's* tradition).[12]

Fundamentalism as such is a modern phenomenon, although belief in the inerrancy of Scripture was of course a common position before the rise of biblical criticism in Europe in the eighteenth and nineteenth centuries. It is a modern phenomenon in that it sees itself in *reaction against* such a modern, 'critical' viewpoint. As such it cannot properly be ascribed to people whose stage of faith is earlier than Stage 3, which is the stage at which abstract, ordered thinking is in place.

The conforming stage (Stage 3) fits in well with some of the understandings of authority of certain fundamentalist Churches. But a 'self-chosen' fundamentalism, in which there is a deliberate adoption of fundamentalist ways, is clearly a Stage 4 phenomenon. It is very unlikely that the more open and plural style of knowing distinctive of Stage 5 could ever be described as fundamentalist. For this reason Fowler's faith stage analysis might appear to some to be unsympathetic to fundamentalism (and sympathetic to at least some forms of liberalism?), at least as a final form of fully adult faith.

In this and many other areas the role of authority figures is crucial. Issues of dependency, individual rebellion and the 'authority' status of Scripture, tradition, reason and the clergy are continuing concerns within the Church. Faith development theory may help us to see how—and why—different people at different times rely on authorities for their faithing.

FAITH DEVELOPMENT AND PASTORAL CARE

This is the title of a book by Fowler which has as its twin focus (i) the Christian understanding of human vocation, and (ii) the pattern of care aimed at the maintenance and transformation of community and the rectification, correction, healing, redemption and regeneration of that vocation. Fowler's approach to pastoral care, therefore, places strong emphasis on the intentional efforts congregations make 'to awaken and form persons for their vocations' (*FDPC* 21). Where faith development relates to this theme is in its recognition of 'some of the patterns of struggle, growth, and change that characterize human beings in the process of becoming aware, conscious, and increasingly responsive and responsible selves, as partners with God' (*FDPC* 53). Here faith development theory is seen as a contribution to 'theological anthropology'—i.e. the Christian view of what it is to be human. This may help to counterbalance the much more dominant influence in pastoral care of psychoanalytical psychology by providing a contribution from a more cognitive and developmental approach.

The pastoral care of individuals needs to be informed by as full an account as possible of 'where they are'. Many personal crises result from the disruptive experience of change, and Fowler argues that faith development theory should help us to understand a number of different sorts of change better. In particular, of course, it is relevant to developmental change, the change that results from the maturation and formation of the self, and 'fundamental shifts in the ways that persons construct life' (*CA* 187).

> Development is a process of alternations between times of provisional balance and coming unbalanced, then finding a recovered balance in a new place. (*FDPC* 101)

An important dimension of the pastoral problems of children, young people and adults is often what Fowler calls this 'normal developmental crisis of faith' (*CA* 201).

There is also change that involves conversion and transformation, or the 'reconstruction' of the self to heal past wounds. Faith development theory may help us to understand and stand by people undergoing these radical changes as well. But for very many children and adults the greatest crises will be brought about by 'intrusive events' that precipitate colossal life changes: e.g. bereavement, marriage, divorce (of oneself or one's parents), the birth or adoption of a child, illness, redundancy, or a move of house or job. How we care for people undergoing these sorts of change will depend in part on where they are in their developmental journeys of faith, and where we are in ours. Thus: 'a conversation full of abstract concepts about the afterlife . . . is of no use to a five year old whose parents have just died' (*CA* 188, cf. 201ff).[13]

But pastoral care is not just an orientation to individuals. It is directed also to communities: to families, school classes, youth groups, work and leisure communities—and especially to the worshipping community of the Church. This last, we should recognize yet again, contains a wide range of stages of faith and selfhood. 'All-age' or 'inter-generational' learning, in which children, adolescents and adults are formed and reformed in the Christian faith together, is frequently to be found in the Church—especially through the learning experiences of worship.[14] Those who bear responsibility for organizing worship and for preaching need to be aware of how the liturgy and the sermon affect children and adults at very different faith stages. Here liturgical, educational—and pastoral—concerns should combine in creating a worshipping environment that arouses, deepens and strengthens *everyone's* faith.

HOW THE FAITH STAGE OF TEACHERS/CLERGY MAY AFFECT THEIR TREATMENT OF OTHERS

Concern for the processes of pastoral care inevitably raises this topic. Various issues come to mind here. It is likely that those already at Stage 3 or 4 will try to bring those at a lower stage to Stage 3, provided that they are developmentally 'ready' for it, in whatever way is appropriate in the circumstances. This will be so because of the very nature of these stages. Where Stage 1 or 2 is roughly 'normal' for the age of those concerned, ordinary teaching methods would be appropriate. Where those at Stage 1 or 2 are *adults* some further guidance may be needed. This should take account of the potential capability of the individual concerned and whether he shows adult intelligence in other respects. The question is: 'Should I help this person to move on, and if so how?'. Sensitively reflective pastoral and educational experience is worth its weight in gold in such circumstances.

More difficult problems may arise where clergy or teachers are at Stage 3 or Stage 4, and have to deal with students, parishioners, parents and others who are at—or approaching the point of moving towards— Stage 5, at least in some respects. This is a serious matter for those who carry a particular burden of responsibility for understanding and facilitating the faith development of others in a church context, and especially for senior clergy, Christian education advisers, super-intendents and others.[15] The difficulty is that Stage 3 and Stage 4 people do not see the possibility of anything different from their own position being valid. There is no easy way round this problem, apart from waiting or encouraging further faith development on the part of those in positions of leadership and responsibility. But we have known the problem to be overcome by those who are supremely motivated by love and goodwill (and are usually elderly!). Perhaps love and time have the power to endure and triumph in these areas as well.

FAITH DEVELOPMENT AND DISAGREEMENTS WITHIN THE CHURCH

Stephen Sykes has argued that disagreement is endemic in the Church:

> Conflict in Christianity is not accidental or occasional, but intrinsic and chronic. . . . Diversity . . . is the norm for Christianity.[16]

Faith development theory gives us a useful commentary on at least some forms of theological or religious disagreement. Developmental theory is predictive. When the main details of the sequence are known, it is possible to diagnose the present position and to predict what will come next if there is any change. This information is of great value for clergy, counsellors or teachers. If they understand the sequence they are better able to respond to others on a one-to-one basis, and to make their remarks more appropriate to the immediate need. They may also be more sympathetic towards those who disagree with them. This, however, happens only in one direction, as we have seen. Those who have graduated through several stages can appreciate positions they have left, whereas it is not possible for a person to understand very much ahead of his current standpoint. We know the countryside we have passed through, but we cannot yet recognize what lies ahead. 'It does not yet appear what we shall be.' Thus some contentious figures are better able to understand their opponents' positions than those opponents can understand the people *they* oppose. Those in the early stages can often appreciate only one viewpoint. There is an asymmetry here, which is exacerbated by the fact that the more we understand the greater is our capacity to adjust our modes of expression to fit all the stages through which we have passed. Faith development theory may help us to acknowledge this rather galling situation more easily, and perhaps to live with it with more patience.[17]

WORSHIP

Worship is essentially the expression of (human and religious) faith in our centres of value, images of power and master stories. In Christian worship we express our attitudes to God, Jesus and one another, and that expression also serves to reinforce our trust, devotion and commitment and to evoke it in others. Christian worship is thus a most potent medium through which we learn to be Christian. The 'master story' of the Christian faith, centred on Jesus the Christ, is rehearsed and celebrated in worship. Through this worship the Christian story becomes once again our story, the focus of our faith. Worship is one of the most powerful crucibles for the formation of our faith.[18]

Worship is very frequently an all-age—and an all-stage—experience. Many children in a congregation will be at Stages 1 or 2. Those at Stage 1 will be feeding on, and greatly influenced by, the images and symbols provided by the worship. The sacramental worship of the eucharist provides a vast amount of such imagery—bread and wine, eating and drinking, standing and kneeling, moving to the altar, the colourful clothing of altar and priest, and so on. But 'non-liturgical' worship is also rich in symbolic forms. These include the architecture of the church, the attention paid to the Bible, and the rituals of the taking up of the offering and (very importantly) hymn-singing. The verbal symbols of both forms of worship, particularly the concrete images from the Bible, hymnody and preaching, are also most significant. Stage 2 worshippers, we recall, are more heavily 'into story'. For them meaning will mainly come in story form. It is hard to overestimate the potency of the narratives and parables from the Bible and other worship sources in their nurture.

At these and later stages the worshippers' sense of community with others will be influenced by the way they relate to, and where they fix the boundaries of, their own 'faith communities'. At Stage 4 there may be a distancing from worship and the worshipping community, as its culture is seen 'from the outside'—reflectively and self-critically. Its *symbols* will be translated into *concepts* by a person at Stage 4, and inevitably they will lose some of their power.[19] Its stories will be analyzed and weighed and held at arm's length. Worship may not become a meaningful experience again until there is a decision to 'jump back into the water' of a particular worshipping community, or until the individual has moved to a Stage 5 faith which can appreciate symbols, myths and rituals once more in what Fowler, following Paul Ricoeur, calls a new 'second naivety'.

It is commonplace to comment that the leader of worship needs to recognize that corporate worship must offer something for everyone. The difficulties posed by the diversity of his congregation are compounded by the addition of this diversity of faith stage. But difficulties will be no stranger in this area!

RELEVANCE FOR CHRISTIAN EDUCATION

Faith development theory is not a theory of Christian education. But it does provide us with a deeper understanding of the context of Christian education and of the nature of the Christian learners—and of the teachers of the Christian faith. Exploring the ways in which people know, value and relate to what they believe to be ultimate can help the Christian educator decide how to facilitate the Christian learning of this particular person at this particular stage. We undoubtedly need a rich variety of Christian learning experiences in the Church to accommodate people at all faith stages, and to support and feed them as they move between stages.

A number of areas command our attention under this general heading of the relevance of faith development theory for Christian education.

(1) Language

The comprehensiveness of Anglicanism is partly a result of the Church of England's retaining the traditional language of Scripture, creed and liturgy while accepting that this language is susceptible of interpretation, at least to some extent, according to the individual's own theology—and, we should now add, his own faith stage. Herein lies the value of set liturgical forms of words as well as of rites. Christian education can provide opportunities for people to re-interpret this language according to their capacity, as liturgical seasons and festivals regularly call to mind the great truths that are ripe for such re-interpretation. It is of considerable help to an individual to be provided with a vocabulary *into* which it is possible to grow in the Christian life. It is valuable to have varied ways of saying the same thing. For example traditional words—sin, salvation, heaven, hell—are used. But with accompanying glosses, appropriate to context, new possibilities of meaning can be opened out for people at different faith stages (e.g. 'sin' understood as a kind of paralysis or hindrance in becoming one's true authentic self—cf. Rom 7.14-23, or as a distortion in being as one ought to be). Without these layers or levels of interpretation, and the permission to use them, Christians may be hindered in their personal faith development. This is another example of the interaction of the content and the form of human and Christian faith.

(2) Educating the Christian educators

The idea is often proposed, but less often encouraged, that Sunday school teachers' preparation periods should sometimes include discussion at their own level of how *they* think about some major items of belief or practice. This sort of discussion can help transition to Stages 3 and 4. It certainly gives the teachers confidence in handling Christian language for a variety of ways of putting things, for themselves as well as for children at a variety of stages. The Church owes it to these voluntary teachers to provide them with opportunities to enrich their own style of faith, and often to help them move on to a more adequate faith stage themselves.

The points made above about understanding people at other faith stages are particularly pertinent with regard to the training and support of Christian educators.

(3) Educational opportunities related to faith stages

In addition to the comments made in the text of Chapter 2, we include here some brief notes about appropriate modes of Christian education at the different stages.

Pre Stage 0
This is the stage of 'undifferentiated' faith. We are thinking here of a child under two years old. The conflict between trust and mistrust is very important at this stage, as foundations are laid now for all that follows. Those familiar with the thought of Dr Frank Lake will perhaps

71

recognize parallels with his idea of the first nine months of a child's life as 'the womb of the spirit', in that it is in this period that a trusting relationship needs to be established so that the foundation is laid for faith in later life.

Educational opportunities here lie mainly in the Church's ministry to the family, and need to take unconscious factors into consideration. Parenthood is itself a 'teachable moment' in a couple's life, and new parents may be encouraged then to think about and look for teachable moments throughout the life of their new child, for it is never too soon for Christian education to start—provided that 'education' and 'teachable' are understood in the broadest way possible. Parents also need to reflect on faith formation, and this reflection must include an examination of their own faith. In taking responsibility for their children's faith many adults begin for the first time to reflect seriously about their own, and this is a time when many will move to Stage 4 or beyond.

Outside the family the contexts of the creche or day-care centre are other places where the child should have every opportunity to form trusting relationships. Christian ministers should, and often need to, encourage a valuing and accepting attitude in the congregation both to very young children and to their parents. Church support for parents of children at various stages is an important help to them in their difficult roles as fountainheads of faith.

Stage 1
This is the stage of 'impressionistic' or 'unordered' faith, the age of fantasy when many images are present in the child's mind. We are thinking here of children from two to about seven years. Educational opportunities at this stage abound. It is important that Church education take into account concrete situations in the family and elsewhere where the child's propensity to feed on images and to see the unknown in terms of the known (what has been called 'metaphoric knowing') is taken seriously. Much interesting work can be done with parents on the ritual dimension of home life.

In our work with children in the Church we must start from their experience, using thematic material (e.g. *Steps and Stones*) and the natural 'intuitiveness' of this age, the child's skill of 'knowing by feeling'. Within Christian nurture and school religious education the use of the affective is very important at this stage. We need to encourage children to talk about their feelings about themselves, the person of Jesus, God,

Bible stories, worship, the Church building and so on. Children need to experience and participate in the 'kinaesthetics of worship' from an early stage, thus fostering a sense of belonging. A wide range of educational tactics promote affective learning. They include imaginary journeys, going outside and 'feeling' the atmosphere (developing a sense of creation, and the wonder of God's world etc.), and the technique of 'stilling'.[20]

Stage 2
This is the 'ordering' stage. We are thinking here of children around seven to eleven years, for whom fact is beginning to be separated from fantasy, and for whom narrative has become very significant in their sorting out of a coherent pattern in life and the world. Educational opportunities at this stage are probably related to the child's roles in worship and service more closely than at any other stage. As membership of some organization, club or group is most enthusiastically entered into at this stage, this may provide one of the most potent contexts for Christian education.

In our teaching in school, parish or club this is *the* time to use story, an opportunity to tell the great stories of salvation history. But Stage 2 is also a rather literal stage, and children at this stage will not be able to 'step outside' the narrative and look at it objectively. So we need to exercise some care in our use of biblical stories. This is the time when children are engaged in sorting out real from make–believe. The Church needs to ensure that Jesus isn't thrown out with Father Christmas, a danger that is aggravated by presenting a miraculous Jesus who is indistinguishable from a magical one. Stories of Jesus must be carefully chosen in a 'cross-eyed' fashion: the educator needs to keep one eye on the child's own understanding and one on an adult interpretation of the story's theological value. Parents need particular help in dealing with children's questions at this stage. The Church should also be preparing them to support their children through the next stages.

Stage 3
This is the 'confirming' stage of adolescence. Abstract thinking is possible now, and mutual interpersonal perspective-taking takes place for the first time. Conformity can mean 'making meaning with others', though the values, norms and expectations will be those of the young person's community taken over unexamined. Authority at this stage

is vested in 'they', the significant others. Above all this is the stage where relationships with others are vitally important.

Educational opportunities here lie in any form of youth ministry. Young people may be encouraged to be 'socially aware' by helping them reflect on social issues and institutions. This is a time when they will often enthusiastically get involved with 'causes', provided that these are appropriately presented. The Church should be providing opportunities for youngsters at Stage 3 to talk with adults so as to help them discover their own identity, and to begin in a new way to make sense of life. We need properly to honour this adolescent hunger for reflection and meaning-making, and this quest for the 'holy grail' of the true self.

Adolescents need help and space to learn new modes of prayer, including meditation and contemplative prayer. A new value will be found in silence and directed meditation on scriptural imagery at this stage, both of which may be experienced in a retreat context. This can provide a welcome antidote to the 'clamour of the media' which is particularly directed to young people.

'Where is the theology in what we are doing?' or 'Where is God in all this?' are questions whose answers tend to change this faith stage. Youth workers, clergy and parents need to be ready for such potential changes to a further stage. This is perhaps a time of unexplored opportunity for 'all-age' activities—especially learning and worship. Such events encourage dialogue between the ages: an opportunity to learn from one another which can promote a new openness to change, something which will also tend to move adolescents on to the next stage.

Stage 4
This is the 'deciding' or 'either/or' stage, often reached in young adulthood.[21] The person reaching a Stage 4 mode of operating has two main tasks in front of her:

(i) the formation of a clear 'ideology' of her own, the choice of her own set of beliefs; and

(ii) allowing an 'executive ego' to emerge—where the self is not just the sum of the roles one carries out, but is expressed through those roles (although relationships continue to be important). So, in introducing oneself, a typical statement would now be not 'I'm a housewife' or 'I'm a civil servant', but 'I'm Joan', 'I'm John', etc.

When considering educational opportunities we should recall that people at this stage are not particularly open to those who are different from them. They often succumb to the temptation to caricature positions other than their own. This needs to be kept in mind when drawing up educational programmes.

Kieran Egan would put Stage 4 into his 'Philosophic Stage' of educational development,[22] a time for reflection and belief-espousal. People in transition from Stage 3 to Stage 4 need particular help in 'building their own ideology', in constructing their own set of beliefs. It is during this time that many people will first find and form their sense of vocation, discovering/deciding what their peculiar purpose and role in life might be. Key questions now are 'What is my gift?', 'Where am I drawn to be in the world?'. Sharon Parks writes about the Stage 3 to 4 transition using the image of someone pushing away from the dock 'of that which has been sure moorage, to move out into the deep waters of exploring for oneself what is true and trustworthy'.[23] At first a paddle must be used, but then the stream takes the canoe and the young adult no longer needs to exert his own force. This analogy of the Spirit, immanent in human life and development, is a useful corrective to our parental and ecclesiastical concerns for the developing faith of our grown-up children.

The Church should be encouraging people at this stage to mix widely, to get involved in dialogue and discussion, and so to come to accept that there are positions other than their own. This should help to prevent the confusion of statements of doctrine with that to which they point—a confusion which is one of the dangers of Stage 4. It might also lead, as and when development allows, to a proper move to the next stage of faith.

Stage 5

This is the 'balanced' stage, when the clear recognition that 'I don't have all the truth' appears for the first time. People at this stage are open to the perspectives of other groups, and are able to engage in dialogue with those who are 'different'—even with our enemies and those who have previously been too threatening. There is also a deeper sense of self and of the fragility of life. Many will have been through some sort of 'mid-life crisis' in which an earlier sense of self, vocation and purpose has broken down. So this is a time of rebuilding vocations, images of self, and faith. Perhaps most important of all this is the stage of 'both/and', when opposing views can be held together in a new creative tension.

People at this stage have been exposed to a variety of different viewpoints and have begun to examine them sympathetically. They are also able to look at the limitations and strengths of their own faith positions. Educational opportunities should be provided for those at Stage 5 to *intensify* their religious affinities. People in transition from Stage 4 to 5 sometimes need to have anomalies deliberately introduced so as to help them look critically at their own beliefs. But we also need to heed the warning expressed elsewhere: we all knit our own shawl of meaning, and we should not slash at another's. The value of 'the journal' and other means of stimulating autobiographical reflection is enormous at this stage (cf. the *Unfolding Tapestry Exercise* in the Appendix of this book). Whereas at Stage 4 the person tends to look critically at mythology and symbolism, at Stage 5 these things have a new power to bring insights to prayer, worship and belief.

We should strive to use Stage 5 people more in our churches—as voluntary teachers, people to lead study groups and in various other unofficial and official Church ministry roles. Very often such individuals are marginalized by Church officials because their very openness makes them suspect and difficult to categorize. In truth, however, they can make the very best sort of Christian educator— one who has walked the same road before us, and in front of us.

THEOLOGICAL TRAINING

The 'training' (formation and education) of clergy and ministers may be helpfully informed by faith development thinking. Two particular points are worth stressing.

A proper practical training of the clergy should include some real experience of real people at different faith stages. Parish placements, hospital visiting and school contacts are essential to provide this range of experience. Just listening to and talking with children, young people and adults of a variety of ages is one of the most valuable preparations for a practical Christian ministry of word and sacrament—of caring, leading worship, preaching and teaching. If this wide experience of people along the way of faith can be reflected upon and discussed with other students and teachers, then the value of the experience will be enormously enhanced.

Time spent at theological college, or on a non-residential training course, is itself likely to prove to be a time of faith development for those in training. Very often it is a 'leaving home' experience as men and women come out of a particular congregation, family or educational context into a community that is often made up of a greater diversity of 'faiths'. A move from Stage 4 to Stage 5—and in some cases from Stage 3 to Stage 4—may thus be accelerated by entering theological education. Students in colleges might do well to take account of such faith-movements in their own lives and those of their fellow students. For similar reasons, teachers and chaplains who are charged with the pastoral care and training of these ordinands may find the faith development analysis useful in their own work. This latter group should comprise people who show spiritual maturity, having learned something themselves of the 'wisdom of time'. However theological education is understood, it needs staff with real faith maturity as well as intellectual (theological) prowess. Recruiting bright young scholars as teachers in theological colleges may not be the only or the best strategy to ensure this situation. Our earlier remarks would suggest that those mentors who are at Stage 5 will find it easiest to understand students who are at other faith stages.

In *Life Maps* Sam Keen writes of the true theological educator (modelled on the *'shaman'* rather than the 'priest', one who 'has the courage to go into the depths') as a person who 'talks out of his own experience rather than gossiping about other people's experience'. 'Seminary education', he adds indignantly, 'consists largely of gossiping about religious experience' (*LM* 155). If this is so, it is a grievous fault.

Conclusion: The Journey Continues

Our journey through the faith development literature and its implications has been a short one, although it will already be regarded as too long by some. We will conclude briefly.

We have attempted here to introduce faith development theory in a way that we trust has been fairly gentle on the understanding, without being grossly unfair to its own intellectual subtleties or those of its critics. There is doubtless much that has been left unsaid that should have been said both for and against this 'Grand Hypothesis'. At the very least we hope to have encouraged people to read and reflect further for themselves, and perhaps to find some illumination for their own work and faith.

Some will have journeyed with us thus far only to reject the qualified endorsement that we are offering faith development theory. 'There is something in it', we have said, when at our most tentative. Most of the members of this Working Party have expressed much more enthusiasm for the theory than that. Some readers will deny even that much. So the debate will continue. As educators with a concern for truth and for Christian faith, we hope that that debate will continue to bear fruit. Whatever one's position on the questions raised and the answers given in this book, Christians owe it to themselves to reflect on what it is we are about in the human activity that we call 'faith'. And it is to all those who are called to arouse, preserve, deepen, enrich, nourish, catalyze, goad, educate and strengthen this human and Christian faith, that this essay is dedicated.

Before dropping this theme, and concluding this text, we should note Fowler's own evaluation of the place of faith development in the teaching and caring ministry of the Church:

> It probably is not helpful to think of stage transition or development from one stage to another as the direct goal of pastoral care, preaching, or Christian education. Our first concern, of course, is the proclamation of the gospel and the attempt to help it find a deep and firm rooting in the soil of people's lives. Next we are concerned about the awakening and shaping of vocation in accordance with an understanding of partnership with the action of God. If we are

faithful in the pastoral leadership relating to these tasks, faith development, as a movement from one stage to another, will come as byproduct and fruit of our common work and that of the Spirit. (*FDPC* 81)

Notes

1 What is Faith?

[1] The vignettes printed in this book mainly originate in 'faith development interviews' conducted by the Revd Derek Atkinson and Dr Marion Smith. The names have been changed throughout. 'Jane' showed a number of Stage 6 characteristics, for details of the faith stages see Chapter 2.

[2] References to Fowler's works are cited in this form. For a key to the abbreviations see the list on piv and the Bibliography, p89.

[3] See especially Wilfred Cantwell Smith, *The Meaning and End of Religion* (Macmillan, New York, 1963), chs 6 and 7, and *Faith and Belief* (Princeton University Press, Princeton, New Jersey, 1979), ch 1. Fowler also draws on the writings of other theologians and students of religion, particularly H. Richard Niebuhr, but also Paul Tillich and occasionally Richard R. Niebuhr and Bernard Lonergan.

[4] S. Parks, *The Critical Years: The Young Adult Search for a Faith to Live By* (Harper & Row, San Francisco, 1986), pp21 and 26.

[5] A somewhat different account is given by H. Richard Niebuhr, and is drawn on by Fowler. See J. Fowler, *To See the Kingdom* (Abingdon, New York, 1974), ch V, and *SF* 19ff.

[6] Cf. below p37f.

[7] It is sometimes argued that Fowler's Stage 6 differs from his Stage 5 in content only, and not at all in its structure of faith-knowing. See G. Moran, *Religious Education Development* (Winston Press, Minneapolis, Minnesota, 1983), pp118ff. Compare Fowler's comments in *LM* 90.

[8] The following, more detailed, account of how the same (or a similar) image of God might look in different forms of faith is based on the Working Party's researches. (For details of the stages see Chapter 2.)
The Stage 2 'form' of faith statement might be something like:
 'God is such a nice person . . .',
where the image is a simple one relating to such 'story' as had come this person's (probably young person's) way, and is understood literally.
Stage 3 might produce something like:
 'Three persons in one trinity—as my minister says . . .',
where the person 'takes over' this statement unexamined.
Stage 4 enables the person to reason about statements, accepting some and rejecting others, but not warming to the views of other people:
 'Either Christ is God or he isn't. I choose to believe that he is, with all that follows.'
Stage 5 people are ready to listen to others' truth:
 'God is the God of Anglicans, Methodists, Orthodox, Catholics, and we need to learn from them something of how they see the truth about God . . .'

Stage 6 people tend to remove all barriers between people, so:
'God is not just a possession of Christians—God is still God whether we call
ourselves Christians, Jews, Muslims, Hindus . . .'

⁹ Overheard conversations with infants. The last item is adapted from J. Hughes,
Will my Rabbit go to Heaven?—And Other Questions Children Ask (Lion, Tring, 1988),
p46.

¹⁰ Cf. Jean Piaget, *Six Psychological Studies* (Random House, New York, 1967). For
an introductory survey see M. Brearley and E. Hitchfield, *A Teacher's Guide to
Reading Piaget* (Routledge & Kegan Paul, London, 1966). For references to criticisms
of Piaget's work see below note 24 to chapter 3.

¹¹ R. Goldman, *Religious Thinking from Childhood to Adolescence* (Routledge & Kegan
Paul, London, 1964), especially ch 4. For a survey of criticisms of Goldman, and
of the Piagetian stage model, see N. Slee, 'Goldman yet again', *British Journal of
Religious Education,* 8, 2 (1986). A comprehensive survey of research on religious
thinking and ideas of God is to be found in K. E. Hyde, *Religion in Childhood and
Adolescence* (Religious Education Press, Birmingham, Alabama, 1990), chs 1-4. John
Hull's slim volume, *God-talk with Young Children: Notes for Parents and Teachers*
(University of Birmingham, Birmingham and CEM, Derby, 1991) provides
illustrative material from conversations with children with illuminating comments.

¹² Because we are beginning with this aspect of faith, and because Fowler's account
is often criticized for overstressing the cognitive dimensions of faith over against
the affective (feeling) ones, it is worth making two points here.

Firstly, Fowler regards changes in the way of thinking as a necessary, but not
a sufficient, condition of change from one faith stage to the next (because this change
is essential to changes in perspective-taking and moral judgement)—cf. *FSM* 76,
LM 39f. But a change in the level of thinking might occur without a faith stage
change. .

The second point is that Fowler treats Piaget's sort of knowing ('a logic of rational
certainty') as part of a more complex, comprehensive, inclusive and primitive 'logic
of conviction' which is the form knowing takes in faith (*FDF* 23, 33). The latter
is like the trunk of a tree 'nurtured by roots of experience, intuition, feeling,
imagination and judgement'. The former is one of its principal branches—emerging
'as a narrowing and specialization of this broader knowing and reasoning' (*FDF*
286f). Thus the logic of rational certainty, which leads to self-critical, objective
knowing, is to be found *within* the more comprehensive processes of the logic of
conviction (the other aspects of faith). We might say that rationality forms a part
of passionate commitment. 'Reasoning in faith' involves a balanced interaction
between the two ways of structuring knowledge (*SF* 103).

¹³ More recently Fowler has questioned this view claiming (with Daniel Stern) that
the child has an inchoate sense of its difference from the rest of its environment
from the beginning. See Fowler *FDEC* 6ff and D. N. Stern, *The Interpersonal World
of the Infant* (Basic Books, New York, 1985), part II.

¹⁴ See Kohlberg's 'Stage and sequence: The cognitive developmental approach to
socialization' in D. A. Goslin (ed), *Handbook of Socialization Theory and Research* (Rand

McNally, Chicago, 1969) and his essay (ch 30) in S. and C. Modgil (eds), *Lawrence Kohlberg: Consensus and Controversy* (Falmer Press, Lewes, 1985). For references to criticisms of Kohlberg see below Chapter 3, note 17 and note 24.

15 Luke 10:29.

16 Fowler talks of a shawl of meaning that we wrap round ourselves, but must later discard, knitting ourselves a new one. See above p41.

17 Compare Sam Keen on 'the wisdom of time', quoted above p56f.

18 William Golding, describing the power of symbols for himself as a child, writes: 'I know about symbols without knowing that I know. . . . I have never heard of levels of meaning, but I experience them. In my notebook, the scarab, the ankh, the steps, the ladder, the thet, are drawn with a care that goes near to love' ('Egypt from my inside', in his *A Moving Target,* Faber & Faber, London, 1982, p47).

2   When is Faith?

1 See E. H. Erikson, *Childhood and Society* (Granada, London, 1977), ch 7. Most of the material in this and the next few paragraphs is from Marion Smith's article 'Developments in faith', *The Month* (July 1983).

2 Selman, who has concentrated on detailed empirical testing in his work on perspective-taking, describes his own 'levels' of social perspective as 'painted with impressionistic brush strokes rather than with the style and stroke of the absolutely clear-cut, photographic empiricist portrait painter'. R. L. Selman, *The Growth of Interpersonal Understanding* (Academic Press, New York, 1980), p80. See also J. H. Flavell, *Cognitive Development* (Prentice-Hall, Englewood Cliffs, New Jersey, 1985), pp291ff.

3 See R. Kegan, *The Evolving Self* (Harvard University Press, Cambridge, MA, 1982); and his essay 'There the dance is: Religious dimensions of a development framework', in J. Fowler and A. Vergote (eds), *Toward Moral and Religious Maturity* (Silver Burdett, Morristown, New Jersey, 1980).

4 E. Erikson, *Childhood and Society,* pp222ff. Compare P. L. Berger, *A Rumour of Angels* (Penguin, Harmondsworth, 1970), pp71ff; H. Küng, *Does God Exist?* (Random House, New York, 1981), pp442ff.

5 S. Parks, *The Critical Years,* p76.

6 Cf. M. Polanyi, *Personal Knowledge* (Routledge & Kegan Paul, London, 1962), and 'The logic of tacit inference', *Philosophy,* XLI, 155 (1966).

7 J. M. Hull, *What Prevents Christian Adults from Learning?* (SCM, London, 1985), p67. Cf. M. Polanyi, *The Tacit Dimension* (Doubleday, New York, 1967), p18.

8 D. Day and P. May, *Teenage Beliefs* (Lion, Oxford, 1991), p62.

9 Originally we were going to call this the stage of 'Open Faith', but Fowler asked us to consider a different name, himself suggesting 'Balanced Faith' or 'Inclusive Faith'. We found his argument persuasive, and worth repeating:

'Open' too easily translates into 'relativistic'—a refusal or inability to make discriminating judgements between truth claims, aesthetic qualities, or ethical principles or goals. . . . A window stuck open is as useless as a window stuck shut—in either case you have lost the effectiveness of the window. (Personal communication, September 1990.)

10 The polarities within the self include those of one's youth and age, the masculine and feminine within us, the conscious and unconscious elements of the self, and the positive and destructive elements of one's nature—particularly our 'dark side' or 'shadow-self'.

11 But there is some evidence that those who have suffered profound experiences may enter this stage—like Stage 5—at an earlier age.

12 Here Fowler is quoting from his earlier paper 'Perspectives on the family', but in *PF* 14 the text reads 'Life is both loved and held too loosely'. Perhaps this version (misprint?) neatly captures *our* view of the Stage 6 person.

13 The phrase is from Oliver Wendell Holmes: 'I do not give a fig for the simplicity on this side of complexity. But I would give my life for the simplicity on the other side of complexity.'

14 That is: 'a parallel increase in the certainty and depth of selfhood, making for qualitative increases in intimacy with self-others-world' (*SF* 274).

15 The diagram is reprinted from *Emerging Issues in Religious Education* (p200), with permission.

3   Is this Faith?

1 Craig Dykstra, in C. Dykstra and S. Parks (eds), *Faith Development and Fowler* (Religious Education Press, Birmingham, Alabama, 1986), p56. The problems arising from the split between structure and content are commented on by Sharon Parks in the same book (pp143ff).

2 W. C. Smith, *Faith and Belief,* pp7, 142.

3 Cf. J. H. Fernhout's essay in *Faith Development and Fowler* (ch 3). For Lutheran and Reformed perspectives on Fowler's understanding of faith see the articles by W. O. Avery and R. R. Osmer in the journal *Religious Education,* 85, 1 (1990).

4 Both H. Richard Niebuhr and Wilfred Cantwell Smith write of the truly faithless person who has no confidence in any centre of value, no loyalty to any cause, finds no meaning and has lost all hope. See H. R. Niebuhr, *Radical Monotheism* (Faber & Faber, London, 1943), p24; W. C. Smith, *Faith and Belief,* p20. However it is unlikely that any person could be so utterly without faith.

5 W. H. Clark in M. Strommen (ed), *Research in Religious Development* (Hawthorn, New York, 1971), p531.

6 Cf. W. Conn, *Christian Conversion* (Paulist Press, New York, 1986), pp27, 32, 156-157, 208-210 and *passim.* Also R. M. Moseley, 'Faith development and

conversion in the catechumenate', in R. D. Duggan (ed), *Conversion and the Catechumenate* (Paulist, Mahwah, New Jersey, 1984) and R. M. Moseley, *Religious Transformations* (forthcoming).

[7] Cf. V. B. Gillespie, *Religious Conversion and Personal Identity* (Religious Education Press, Birmingham, Alabama, 1979).

[8] S. D. McLean, in *Faith Development and Fowler,* p166.

[9] In passing we may note the rather different implications of the famous remark of Kierkegaard that faith is a risky business, a matter of venturing out far from shore, 'out upon the deep, over seventy thousand fathoms of water' (*Concluding Unscientific Postscript,* trans D. F. Swenson and W. Lowrie (Princeton University Press, Princeton, New Jersey, 1941), p182).

[10] But compare McClean's view, above p39.

[11] Cf. J. M. Hull, *What Prevents Christian Adults from Learning?,* especially ch 3.

[12] R. Marstin, *Beyond Our Tribal Gods: The Maturing of Faith* (Orbis, Maryknoll, New York, 1979), p34. For a perceptive comment and critique of this claim in Kohlberg's work see Don Locke's essay 'A psychologist among the philosophers', in S. and C. Modgil (eds), *op. cit.,* pp27ff, 37f.

[13] Compare the comments by Jack Seymour in J. L. Seymour and D. E. Miller (eds), *Contemporary Approaches to Christian Education* (Abingdon, Nashville, 1982), p25.

[14] Cf. S. D. McLean in *Faith Development and Fowler,* pp162ff, 170f.

[15] S. D. McLean, *op. cit.,* p158; cf. S. Parks, in *Faith Development and Fowler,* p143.

[16] *SF* 296ff. Cf. C. Bruning and K. Stokes: 'the literature on human development is heavily biased toward purely cognitive, rationalistic conceptions of growth. . . . [it] is also biased in the direction of liberalism. It champions tolerance and flexibility over conservative adherence to absolute truths' (K. Stokes (ed), *Faith Development in the Adult Life Cycle* (W. H. Sadlier, New York, 1982), p28; cf. also ch 9). See also J. M. Broughton in *Faith Development and Fowler,* pp95ff.

[17] Carol Gilligan argues that Kohlberg's theory reflects a sexist bias towards autonomy, separateness and independence—cf. her *In a Different Voice* (Harvard University Press, Cambridge, MA and London, 1982), pp18ff. Fowler's results also seem to 'favour' men. His account of Stage 3/4 transition places greater weight on (apparently) 'rational' and 'distanced' choosing than some students of women's faith would recognize. Stabilization at Stage 3 may also fit the life-style of many women better than their male counterparts of the same age. See also M. F. Belenky *et al., Women's Ways of Knowing: The Development of Self, Voice, and Mind* (Basic Books, New York, 1986).

[18] *Faith Development and Fowler,* ch 8.

[19] Their criticisms include (i) the fact that the sample is not necessarily a representative one (but it is a fairly broad one), (ii) doubts about the bias of the interviewers (an inevitable criticism of all interview work), (iii) the generality and abstraction of

the constructs being measured (which does make it difficult to point to precise evidence of their existence), (iv) the wide-ranging nature of the hypothesis, e.g. that faith is a human universal (but every part of the theory is not dependent on such large-scale claims), (v) the uncertain meaning of some of the terms used in the questions (something which can be clarified during the interview), (vi) the limitations of single interviews by relatively untrained interviewers to provide psychoanalytic data (but this does not invalidate the whole work), (vii) the complexity of the problem of scoring and interpreting the interview results (admitted, but the complexity is inevitable), and (viii) the large number of unproven assumptions involved (but all research takes some assumptions on trust).

[20] Such falsifiability is a property essential to any scientific theory.

[21] J. L. Elias, *Psychology and Religious Education* (Catechetical Communications, Bethlehem, Pennsylvania, 1979), p122, cf. pp128ff.

[22] Cf. 'There the dance is', pp406f.

[23] Kohlberg in B. Munsey (ed), *Moral Development, Moral Education and Kohlberg* (Religious Education Press, Birmingham, Alabama, 1980), p40.

[24] Cf. D. Heywood, 'Piaget and faith development: A true marriage of minds?', *British Journal of Religious Education*, 8, 2 (1986). Critics of Fowler often point to his somewhat uncritical use of Piaget and Kohlberg, researchers whose own work is often subject to criticism. It is said, for example, that Piaget underrated the cognitive capacities of young children. See M. Donaldson, *Children's Minds* (Collins, Glasgow, 1978), and Olivera Petrovich, 'An examination of Piaget's theory of childhood artificialism' (DPhil thesis, University of Oxford, 1988). Others argue that many adults engage in formal reasoning only when they are thinking about some subjects and not others (thus content and form are not easily separable). In fact Piaget admitted that people selectively use formal reasoning, depending on their interest, experience or specialization. Both Piaget and Kohlberg are concerned with our *capacity* to reach a particular quality of reasoning, and not with the *extent to which* that ability is actually employed. For a useful account of 'Piaget's contribution to understanding cognitive development' see Sara Meadow's essay in K. Richardson and S. Sheldon (eds), *Cognitive Development to Adolescence* (Open University/Lawrence Erlbaum, Hove, 1988).

With regard to moral development, other critics have commented that there is a serious divergence between what a person thinks or says in moral matters (their 'moral judgements') and how they actually behave—and indeed how they think about real, as opposed to hypothetical, dilemmas. Underlying such criticism may be the mistaken view that complexity of moral reasoning is a measure of the 'moral' person. There can be complex moral reasoning on both sides of a dilemma. With the development of abstract thought there is at least more chance of resistance to outside (bad?) influences on moral decisions. Our moral judgements themselves are often said to depend as much on the particular situations we are in as they do on the way we think morally, but this does not invalidate theories of the development of forms of moral thinking.

It is sometimes remarked that a person who is scored at a particular moral—or faith—stage often shows responses characteristic of other stages as well. Such stage mixture is common, and scoring depends on the balance of responses at each stage. As we have already noted, many psychologists argue that psychological development should now be understood more as a matter of general progression than as a sequence of distinct stages separated by distinct transitional periods. But it seems to us that the difference here is more one of degree or emphasis than a difference in kind.

25 See the research of the Religious Experience Research Unit, e.g. A. Hardy, *The Spiritual Nature of Man* (Clarendon Press, Oxford, 1979); E. G. Robinson, *The Original Vision* (Religious Experience Research Unit, Oxford, 1977); D. Hay, *Religious Experience Today* (Mowbray, London, 1990).

26 Earlier 'developmental' schemes may be traced in other writers on theological and spiritual matters. Reference is sometimes made in this context to the writings of Friedrich von Hügel. Compare *The Mystical Element of Religion* (Dent, London, 1908), ch II and G. Rummery and D. Lundy, *Growing into Faith* (Darton, Longman & Todd, London, 1982), ch 3.

27 J. H. Westerhoff, *Will Our Children Have Faith?* (Seabury Press, New York, 1976), pp89ff.

28 J. H. Westerhoff, *Building God's People* (Seabury Press, New York, 1983), pp44ff. Cf. also his final essay in J. H. Westerhoff and O. C. Edwards (eds), *A Faithful Church* (Morehouse-Barlow, Wilton, Connecticut, 1981), pp300f.

29 This is perhaps rather stretching the metaphor, for embarking on a new trail often involves completely re-tracing one's steps on the present path. In real life trails are not available 'at any time', or 'in any order'!

30 G. Moran, *Religious Education Development,* p197.

31 Other, more carefully researched, accounts of faith development exist that are more closely related to, but offer some detailed qualifications of, Fowler's scheme. One of the most interesting of these is Sharon Parks's *The Critical Years,* which distinguishes a separate stage of the 'young adult' corresponding to Fowler's transition between Stages 3 and 4. Fritz Oser's 'Stages of religious judgment', however, relate only to cognitive patterns of religious knowing (see his essay in *Toward Moral and Religious Maturity*).

4 How is Faith?

1 Leroy T. Howe, 'A developmental perspective on conversion', *Perkins Journal* (Fall 1979), p31.

2 Gordon Wakefield, *A Dictionary of Christian Spirituality* (SCM, London, 1983), p361.

3 See above p72f and footnote 20 below. The College of St Mark and St John, Plymouth has produced a useful video and supplementary materials relevant to this theme entitled *Educating for Spiritual Growth* (Marjon, Plymouth, 1989).

4 Cf. J. H. Westerhoff, *Building God's People,* p75; W. H. Willimon, *Worship as Pastoral Care* (Abingdon, Nashville, 1979), pp122f; G. K. Neville and J. H. Westerhoff, *Learning Through Liturgy,* (Seabury Press, New York, 1978); R. L. Browning and

R. A. Reed, *The Sacraments in Religious Education and Liturgy* (Religious Education Press, Birmingham, Alabama, 1985).

5 The late James Hopewell, a colleague of Fowler at Emory University, Atlanta, has made a substantial contribution in his *Congregation: Stories and Structures* (ed B. G. Wheeler, SCM, London, 1987). Cf. also Jackson W. Carroll *et al.* (eds), *Handbook for Congregational Studies* (Abingdon, Nashville, Tennessee, 1986).

6 It may be, however, that the leaders of these churches are at a different stage. See above p67f.

7 Cf. Fowler *FDEC* 131ff and his forthcoming *Weaving the New Creation* (Harper & Row, San Francisco).

8 Cf. E. A. Carter and M. McGoldrick (eds), *The Changing Family Life Cycle* (Allyn & Bacon, Boston, 1989).

9 Cf. H. Anderson, *The Family and Pastoral Care* (Fortress, Philadelphia; SPCK, London, 1984), pp60ff.

10 *Will our Children Have Faith?*, p53.

11 Cf. J. Barr, *Fundamentalism* (SCM, London, 1981) and A. Peshkin, *God's Choice: The Total World of a Fundamentalist Christian School* (University of Chicago Press, Chicago and London, 1986).

12 R. P. C. Hanson, 'Tradition', in A. Richardson and J. Bowden (eds), *A New Dictionary of Christian Theology* (SCM, London, 1983), p574.

13 For further reflections on faith development and pastoral care see M. Jacobs, *Towards the Fullness of Christ* (Darton, Longman & Todd, London, 1988), especially pp100f and 125ff.

14 Cf. J. W. White, *Intergenerational Religious Education* (Religious Education Press, Birmingham, Alabama, 1988), pp46ff, 148ff, and *Leaves on the Tree: All-Age Learning and Worship, Resources and Reflections* (National Society/Church House Publishing, London, 1990).

15 See N. Emler in H. Weinreich-Haste and D. Locke (eds), *Morality in the Making* (Wiley, Chichester, 1983), p64. He points out that those who adhere to the norms themselves (as both Stage 3 and 4 do in their own ways) will view those who think differently as 'law-breakers or enemies of the social system who must be punished, constrained, or ejected'. 'Such a view is only morally inappropriate to one who believes there are defensible alternatives or moral objections to the social order.' (Emler is writing about morality and politics but there are obvious parallels in the sphere of religion.)

16 S. W. Sykes, *The Identity of Christianity* (SPCK, London, 1984), p52.

17 Don Cupitt offers some useful comments on a related issue (conservative/radical disagreements) in his *Life Lines* (SCM, London, 1986), pp204f, a book that offers some radical reflections on various religious stations along a 'Metro map of the Spirit'.

[18] Cf. note 4 above.

[19] See the anecdote about Harvey Cox and his demythologizing girlfriend in *SF* 180f.

[20] Stilling is a way in to meditation and worship. Children are encouraged to stop all other activity for a while in order to be still, to reflect on and respond to an inner awareness of 'worth-ship' in, for example, a moment of 'peace', 'harmony', 'light', 'oneness', 'beauty', 'concern for others', etc. Through stilling children can be introduced to some of the basic ingredients of prayer, especially a sense of inner quietness, listening and receptivity. This technique can of course also apply to other stages, as can various methods of experiential religious education. See M. Beesley, *Stilling: A Pathway for Spiritual Learning in the National Curriculum* (Salisbury Diocesan Board of Education, Salisbury, 1990), and J. Hammond *et al, New Methods in RE Teaching: An Experiential Approach* (Oliver & Boyd, Harlow, 1990).

[21] We should, however, recall that a significant number of people make the transition to Stage 4 in their thirties or forties, and some never do so. Similarly a good number of adults remain in the 'adolescent' Stage 3.

[22] K. Egan, *Educational Development* (Oxford University Press, New York, 1979), ch 3.

[23] S. Parks, *The Critical Years,* p55.

Booklist

1. SOME WORKS BY JAMES FOWLER

BABC   *Becoming Adult, Becoming Christian* (Harper & Row, San Francisco, 1984).

CA   J. W. Fowler and R. Osmer, 'Childhood and adolescence—A faith development perspective', in R. J. Wicks, R. D. Parsons and D. E. Capps (eds), *Clinical Handbook of Pastoral Counseling* (Paulist, New York, 1985).

EIRE   'Faith development theory and the aims of religious socialization', in G. Durka and J. Smith (eds), *Emerging Issues in Religious Education* (Paulist Press, New York, 1976).

FDEC   'Strength for the journey: Early childhood development in selfhood and faith' and 'The public Church: Ecology for faith education and advocate for children', in D. Blazer (ed), *Faith Development in Early Childhood* (Sheed & Ward, Kansas City, 1989).

FDF   'Faith and the structuring of meaning' and 'Dialogue towards a future in faith development studies', in C. Dykstra and S. Parks (eds), *Faith Development and Fowler* (Religious Education Press, Birmingham, Alabama, 1986).

FDPC   *Faith Development and Pastoral Care* (Fortress Press, Philadelphia, 1987).

FSM   'Faith and the structuring of meaning', in J. Fowler and A. Vergote (eds), *Toward Moral and Religious Maturity* (Silver Burdett, Morristown, New Jersey, 1980).

G   'Faith, liberation and human development', *The Foundation* (Gammon Theological Seminary, Atlanta), 79 (1974).

LM   J. Fowler and S. Keen, *Life Maps: Conversations on the Journey of Faith* (Winston Press, Minneapolis, Minnesota, and Word Books, Waco, Texas, 1978).

M   R. M. Moseley, D. Jarvis, and J. W. Fowler, *Manual for Faith Development Research* (Center for Faith Development, Emory University, Atlanta, Georgia, 1986).

MSDF   'Moral stages and the development of faith', in B. Munsey (ed), *Moral Development, Moral Education and Kohlberg* (Religious Education Press, Birmingham, Alabama, 1980).

N   'Faith development through the family life cycle', *Network Paper No. 31* (Don Bosco Multimedia, New Rochelle, New York, no date).

PF   'Perspectives on the family from the standpoint of faith development theory', *The Perkins Journal*, 33, 1 (1979).

SF   *Stages of Faith: The Psychology of Human Development and the Quest for Meaning* (Harper & Row, San Francisco, 1981).

SFALC   'Stages of faith and adults' life cycles', in K. Stokes (ed), *Faith Development in the Adult Life Cycle* (W. H. Sadlier, New York, 1982).

2. SOME WORKS COMMENTING ON FAITH DEVELOPMENT

W. O. Avery, 'A Lutheran examines James W. Fowler', *Religious Education*, 85, 1 (1990).

D. A. Blazer (ed), *Faith Development in Early Childhood* (Sheed and Ward, Kansas City, 1989).

G. L. Chamberlain, *Fostering Faith: A Minister's Guide to Faith Development* (Paulist, Mahwah, New Jersey, 1988).

C. Dykstra and S. Parks (eds), *Faith Development and Fowler* (Religious Education Press, Birmingham, Alabama, 1986).

M. Ford-Grabowsky, 'Flaws in faith development theory', *Religious Education*, 82, 1 (1987).

M. Gorman, 'Moral and faith development in seventeen-year-old students', *Religious Education*, 72, 5 (1977).

T. H. Groome, *Christian Religious Education: Sharing Our Story and Vision* (Harper & Row, New York, 1981), ch 4.

T. C. Hennessy (ed), *Values and Moral Development* (Paulist, New York, 1976; essays by T. C. Hennessy and A. McBride, as well as by Fowler).

D. Heywood, 'Piaget and faith development: A true marriage of minds?', *British Journal of Religious Education*, 8, 2 (1986).

J. M. Hull, *What Prevents Christian Adults from Learning?* (SCM, London, 1985), ch 4.

M. Jacobs, *Towards the Fullness of Christ* (Darton, Longman & Todd, London, 1988).

S. Keen, material in *Life Maps* (see *LM* in Booklist 1).

K. Kürzdörfer, 'From Kohlberg to Fowler—an educational advance?', *Panorama*, 1, 1 (1989). (See also papers by Mokrosch and Schweitzer.)

J. E. Loder and J. W. Fowler, 'Conversations on Fowler's *Stages of Faith* and Loder's *The Transforming Moment*', *Religious Education*, 77, 2 (1982).

G. Moran, *Religious Education Development* (Winston Press, Minneapolis, Minnesota, 1983), ch 6.

R. M. Moseley, 'Faith development and conversion in the catechumenate', in R. Duggan (ed), *Conversion and the Catechumenate* (Paulist, Mahwah, New Jersey, 1984).

R. M. Moseley and K. Brockenbrough, 'Faith development in the preschool years', in D. Ratcliff (ed), *Handbook of Preschool Religious Education* (Religious Education Press, Birmingham, Alabama, 1988).

C. E. Nelson, 'Does faith develop? An evaluation of Fowler's position', *Living Light*, 19 (1982).

R. R. Osmer, 'James W. Fowler and the Reformed tradition', *Religious Education*, 85, 1 (1990).

S. Parks, *The Critical Years: The Young Adult Search for a Faith to Live By* (Harper & Row, San Francisco, 1986).

G. Rummery and D. Lundy, *Growing into Faith* (Darton, Longman & Todd, London 1982).

D. Schurter, 'Fowler's faith stages as a guide for ministry to the mentally retarded', *Journal of Pastoral Care,* 41 (1987).

J. L. Seymour and D. E. Miller (eds), *Contemporary Approaches to Christian Education* (Abingdon, Nashville, 1982), ch 4.

M. E. Smith, 'Developments in faith', *The Month* (July 1983).

M. E. Smith, 'Answers to some questions about faith development', *British Journal of Religious Education,* 8, 2 (1986).

M. E. Smith, 'Progress in faith development', *The Month* (March 1986).

M. E. Smith, 'Vocation and maturity of faith', *The Month* (April 1986).

C. J. Steckel, 'The emergence of morality and faith in stages: A theological critique of developmental theories', in P. W. Pruyser (ed), *Changing Views of the Human Condition* (Mercer University Press, Macon, Georgia, 1987).

K. Stokes (ed), *Faith Development in the Adult Life Cycle* (W. H. Sadlier, New York, 1982).

D. H. Webster, 'James Fowler's theory of faith development', *British Journal of Religious Education,* 7, 1 (1984).

Appendix: Practical Exercises

We reprint here, with the kind permission of James Fowler, two practical exercises which may be used with individuals as a means of encouraging them to reflect on the development of their faith. Please note that these are *not* faith development interviews, and cannot be used to allocate people to different faith stages. Note too that they focus on the content of faith (e.g. 'images of God') as much as on its form. The exercises have been found valuable, however, when used to accompany introductions to the theory of faith development, and with individuals or groups in other educational or pastoral contexts.

1. THE UNFOLDING TAPESTRY EXERCISE

Introduction by James Fowler:

Policies for Distributing the Unfolding Tapestry Exercise

'The Unfolding Tapestry of My Life' is an exercise intended to help people create a narrative of their past experience in a way that allows both ongoing patterns and critical events and turning points to become evident. Going through this exercise can be a powerfully moving experience, especially for people who have never done such self-reflection before. Therefore the exercise is disseminated with several precautions:

1. We ask those who plan to use the Unfolding Tapestry instrument in their class, workshop or whatever to take time, prior to the event, to go through the exercise themselves.
2. At least two hours, total, should be devoted to filling out the form—three hours is best. Time for remembering and writing should be interspersed with breaks during which the auto-biographers can share their insights, if they desire.
3. After the exercise has been completed, care should be taken to provide support for those who may discover that they need help in processing their feelings and insights.
4. Persons should be assured that they are doing this work entirely for themselves. They will not/should not be asked to let others look

at the tapestry, though they may wish to share their learnings or the chapter titles resulting from it.

5. We ask that you keep the copyright designated for the Center for Faith Development visible on the document. This restricts publication of the document by unauthorized persons and enables us to keep the instrument under some control.

The citation for this instrument is: James W. Fowler, *Faith Development and Pastoral Care*, Fortress Press (1987), pp 122-125.

Instructions for Use of the Unfolding Tapestry of My Life

The worksheet which composes the main part of this reflective exercise has been worked out with the help of Gabriel Clark and members of the Center for Faith Development staff. In its background you may see influences of the works of St Ignatius of Loyola, Ira Progoff, Daniel Levinson and Faith Development theory. It provides a way to work with the movements of our lives, enabling us to see the changes and continuities in our important relationships, commitments and experiences. Please take a moment to look at the worksheet (p97), letting it address your mind and imagination. After you have looked the chart over for a moment, turn back to this page for some explanation of the categories across the top of your sheet.

Starting from the left, number the first column, '*Calendar Years from Birth*', from the calendar year of your birth to the present year. If there are a substantial number of years in your life, you may choose to number with intervals of two, three or five years. In the second column titled '*Place*' we are interested in your recording your sense of place in several different dimensions: first of all, the physical space, including the geographical area in which you lived at various periods of your life. But this could also include your economic and social place (in the sense of social class) and your position of economic and political power or vulnerability.

The third column, '*Key Relationships*' refers to those relationships at different points in one's life which have important impact as regards self-image, self-worth, and the maintenance and restoration of the self. This could include family members, friends, sponsors, mentors, enemies, lovers or spouses, teachers, bosses, etc. These persons need not be living presently and you need not have known them personally (i.e. one might have a key relationship with St Augustine through *The Confessions* or with a grandparent who died before one's birth).

The fourth column we call the *'Uses and Directions of the Self'*. This may seem a peculiar way to get at this area, but what we have in mind is this. At the various points in your life you are spending and being spent in a number of different ways. Some of these might include attending school, acquiring skills, discovering and developing talents, undertaking new responsibilities or the initiation of projects. It also may include roles that you have taken on or created and the foci of preparation or learning in which you are engaged.

Then we come to the column which simply asks you to record your *'Age by Year'*. This is simply to provide another chronological reference point for you. Fill it in with the same intervals that you used for the calendar years on the left-hand side.

The column *'Marker Events'* asks you to record those events or times in your life which are turning points for you. These may include moves from one place to another, the death or loss of loved ones, separations or divorces, changes in your status (economic, political or social), catastrophes or emergencies, graced events, conversion experiences, loss of faith, major decisions or choices that you have made. Marker events occur and things are never quite the same again.

'Events and Conditions in Society and World' is a column in which we ask you to register what is going on in the larger world beyond your family or small circle of friends which has an impact upon you and your way of seeing and being in the world. Such events as wartime, depression, the civil rights struggle in the sixties, the assassination of a president or the launching of Sputnik might be such events in the outside world.

The column *'Images of God'* is an invitation for you to try with a brief note or two to indicate your feelings or thoughts or images of God—positive or negative—at various periods of your life. You may also use this to register a sense of God's presence or absence, or of your belief or disbelief at various points. [See also the *Image of God Exercise*—Ed.]

'Centres of Value and Power' refers to the one or two relationships, roles, institutional involvements or objects which had the most value or worth for you in a given period. Put another way, we are asking what persons or things or causes were of such importance to you that they exerted an organizing power on the other values in your life?

The final column, *'Authorities'*, asks the question who or what constituted authority for you at a given period in your life. Another way to put this: to whom or to what did you look for guidance or for the ratification of your decisions or choices or values at a given time in your life? Where were the times of shifting from one source of authority to another?

As you work on the chart, make brief notes to yourself, indicating the insights or thoughts that you have under each of the columns. It is not necessary to fill out the columns in great detail. *You are doing this for no one but yourself,* therefore simply use a shorthand notation system that will help you recall your own insights and memories.

Some things to do after you have filled out the chart

1. Spend some time reflecting upon the tapestry of your life taken as a whole. Feel its movement and its flow, its continuities and discontinuities. For now, forget all that you know about developmental theory, psychological or otherwise. As you look at the tapestry of your life, let yourself think of it as a large drama or play. Thinking of it this way, let yourself feel where the division between acts of your play would naturally fall. You may have as many acts as you need to make the proper divisions between the movements of your life. When you get a feel for where the divisions between the acts should be, place a line at those points in the chart all the way across the page.

2. Now take some time to meditate upon each of those acts. Let the feelings you have about that period of your life come to the surface. If there are feelings of pain or anguish, regard them for what they are, do not judge them or evaluate them or identify with them, but just see the feelings for what they are. After you have spent a time meditating on each of these acts, try to find a metaphor for each one or a symbol or a title, which will portray for you what you feel that act of your life was really about, and what it means. When you have done this to your satisfaction, you will have finished your work with the chart.

This is the unfolding tapestry of your life at this particular time. You may want later today or in the coming days to return to it and work on it further. Or you may wish at some time several years later to repeat this exercise. You will find that the acts you have identified may fall in a different place, and that some of your feelings about the periods of your life may have altered. Thank you for the work you have put into this exercise. We hope it has been worthwhile for you.

© Center for Faith Development

The Unfolding Tapestry of My Life

Calendar Years from Birth	Place—Geographic and Socio-Economic	Key Relationships	Uses and Directions of the Self	Age by Year	Marker Events	Events and Conditions in Society and World	Images of God	Centres of Value and Power	Authorities

2. THE IMAGE OF GOD EXERCISE

1. Draw a picture or symbol that expresses your understanding of God at these points in your life.
2. Jot down brief reflections under the questions next to each box.

My Childhood Image of God

What was going on in your life?

What was important to you and gave your life meaning?

What was faith to you?

What was going on in your life?

What was important to you and gave your life meaning?

What was faith to you?

My Adolescent Image of God

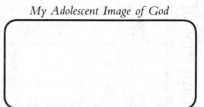

My Present Image of God

What is going on in your life?

What is important to you and gives your life meaning?

What is faith to you?

What about your image of God might be transformed?

What in your life is calling forth this new image of God?

How My Image of God Might Change

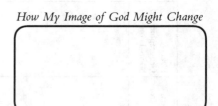

© Center for Faith Development

Index